John H Wellemin

Customer Satisfaction through
TOTAL QUALITY

Chartwell-Bratt   Studentlitteratur

British Library Cataloguing in Publication Data
Wellemin, John H.
    Ensuring customer satisfaction through total quality.
    1. Industries. Quality control.
    I. Titel
    658. 562

ISBN 0-86238-272-6

© John H. Wellemin and Chartwell-Bratt Ltd, 1990

Chartwell-Bratt (Publishing and Training) Ltd
ISBN 0-86238-272-6

Printed in Sweden
Studentlitteratur, Lund
ISBN 91-44-32891-5

| Printing | 1 | 2 | 3 | 4 | 5 | 6 | 7 | 8 | 9 | 10 | 1994 | 93 | 92 | 91 | 90 |

List of Contents

CHAPTER I

Introduction

The reason for existence of any company is to make profit. However, putting profitability as a company's most important corporate value is unlikely to make it highly profitable in the long run. It has been clearly demonstrated that over a period of time the only way a business can stay highly profitable is to satisfy customer needs.

This is obviously an over-simplified statement, as there are many additional components in making a business successful but, stripped to its basics, it is nevertheless true.

Customers have become much more knowledgeable and selective when making their purchasing decisions and we will examine the reasons for this a little later. The quality of the product or service offered is a prerequisite, an entry requirement, for any company that wants to remain successful over the years. The customer is buying a total offering which goes beyond the mere quality of the product or service. He differentiates the various suppliers by the non-product value added he perceives as part of the total offering.

In consequence it has been recognised that it is not only those who produce a product or provide a service to a customer who have to be concerned about quality, but everyone in the company who contributes to the activity of the business in any way. This is a fundamental change in concept which requires a change of attitude throughout the organisation.

Individual functional managers can influence only a part of this process which will have a partial impact on the total customer perception of what is being acquired. To obtain the maximum effect, the whole organisation will have to strive for the same goal of doing its part of the activity as effectively as possible to satisfy the wide variety of customer needs. They are often not clearly identified and may even be contradictory with one another.

It is therefore essential for top management to get involved in driving the total quality and customer care programmes in their companies to ensure a coordinated, clearly defined approach to a goal which must be clearly specified.

The whole purpose of this book is to indicate that only by a clear understanding by every member of an organisation of the reasons for developing this type of programme and where they, as individuals or departments, fit into the overall framework of the activity, will a whole-hearted implementation take place.

This brings me to the first priority of top management:

The Mission Statement

If top management genuinely believe that satisfying customer needs through total quality is of prime importance in achieving its goals, then it is clearly necessary to highlight this in the corporation's mission statement.

The president of one major multi-national corporation changed the priorities in that company's mission statement by elevating "Customer Satisfaction" from the number three to the number one position. In an address to a group of his employees he stated:

> "... we can only achieve our return on assets (ROA) and market share objectives with satisfied customers. The customer is our reason for being".

He then went public with a similar statement which occupied the whole back page of the company's Annual Report, to let everyone know that he was serious about implementing this prioritisation.
Once a business clearly identifies the customer and quality in its "Mission Statement" or "Company Philosophy" it must make sure that this statement or philosophy does not remain mere words – a

statement of this nature must be seen by all its staff and customers to be a way of life in that company.

In too many cases this type of statement is a mere platitude which is not supported by actions and deeds of top management in which case it will quickly lose its validity. Total quality and customer satisfaction will not just happen – companies have to work, and work hard, to achieve results.

This brings me to the next issue we need to discuss:

Communication throughout the Company

Having developed a company philosophy on quality and customer care, it must be communicated throughout the organisation and divisional, departmental and individual standards need to be agreed within the overall goals.

It is a well recognised fact that aspects of a person's job that are targeted and measured will happen. It is usually easier to set a target on the quantity of work rather than agree a desired quality – but it is possible to do so in most situations. This can be done either directly or indirectly and we will discuss this point in more detail in chapter VIII. The point I am trying to make here is that qualitative as well as quantitative standards must be part of the measurement process of a company, if the mission statement is to have any credibility.

The danger exists that staff, having been subjected in the past to various projects which have been abandoned almost as quickly as they had been introduced, will feel that total quality and customer satisfaction programmes will also just be the "flavour of the month". It must be realised by all that this is a continuous company philosophy. It will take a long time to be accepted as a way of life by all members of the company's staff!

This is the reason why most successful programmes are not trying to do everything at once but take the step by step approach of identifying for each group of employees some clear goals and ensure that they are achieved. From the first small step, confidence within the group will be gained and will lead to further successes.

All of us are strongly influenced by the pressure applied on us by our superiors; it is therefore important that the whole process of developing and implementing a customer oriented philosophy in the company is seen to cascade down the organisation, from the chief executive, through his divisional directors, functional managers and supervisors to every member of the staff.

All the issues revolving around quality and customers consist of two separate aspects: the first concerns the identification of the needs, the setting of standards and imparting the necessary skills and knowledge to be able to perform adequately. The second involves the motivation for wanting to do so – this necessitates a positive, customer oriented attitude throughout the company and in chapter IX we will discuss some of the issues involved.

The Role of Top Management

From the last paragraph it will be evident that neither of the two broad aspects mentioned can be adequately driven through an organisation without full participation, direction and control from the top.

It will be necessary to ensure that activities in the various divisions or departments are adequately coordinated to achieve the desired results. This does not mean that top management has to spend a great deal of its time on this coordination process, but top management must ensure that this activity is performed on its behalf and it must review progress and take any necessary decisions.

In the area of changing employee attitudes the role of top management is even more important and its direct involvement needs to be highly visible to all staff. However, it is not the words of management which will make the difference but its actions. Customer considerations must figure in every decision that is taken. This whole issue will be discussed in detail in chapter X.

It is usually much easier for a competitor to copy the features of a product or service than it is to change the attitudes of staff. It takes a great deal of time and persistent and consistent effort to get a customer oriented approach to become an integral part of a company's staff attitude.

The learning process goes through four stages. The first stage is "Unconscious Ignorance" – management and staff do not even realise that some specific action is required to create customer satisfaction or provide high quality support. This could be compared with a small child who is not afraid of deep water because he does not know yet that he needs to know how to swim.

The second stage is "Conscious Ignorance" – management and staff realise that something needs to be done but they are not quite sure what to do or how to do it. The equivalent in our analogy is the child's realisation that it is necessary to learn to swim in order to stay afloat.

In the third stage of "Conscious Knowledge" or "Conscious Skill", management and staff have commenced remedial actions to improve their customer support and total quality but it still requires conscious thinking and effort to make themselves do it. In the case of our young child, he has now learned some of the strokes required to keep him afloat but he has to think what to do to coordinate his movements.

The fourth and last stage moves to "Unconscious Knowledge/Skill", where management and staff have been utilising their customer relation skill and knowledge of how to satisfy customers' needs for some time so that total quality has become second nature to them. An experienced swimmer does not have to think about how to coordinate his arm, leg and head movement with his breathing, it has become quite automatic.

There are no shortcuts; management must involve itself in leading the whole team to acquire all necessary skills and knowledge, provide the necessary facilities and tools, and influence their staff's attitude to recognise that the customer is the source of all company revenues.

CHAPTER II

Historic Background to Quality

When we talked about "Quality" in the past, we invariably thought only of the quality of the product sold to the customer or of the service provided. So let us first look at this aspect of quality.

Product Quality

The quality of a product was thought to be entirely the responsibility of the manufacturing division, with the Chief Inspector making sure that the product which left the factory conformed to a pre-determined standard. The Production Manager was judged more by whether he was able to produce, on schedule and at a low cost, the quantity of items required. Quality was a secondary consideration.

In the seller's market which existed in the post-war years this was a strategy followed by very many companies and the extra costs that this approach incurred was, in the end, paid for by the consumer. And these extra costs were very substantial. Some of them were captured by the company (e.g. warranty costs) but many others were just lost in general overheads.

It is perhaps worthwhile to look at some of the costs incurred due to low quality to understand how companies, who spent a little more effort in evaluating the situation fully, were able to gain an advantage over their competitors in the market place.

Costs rise steeply as we build faulty components into a larger module or sub-assembly, which in turn is built into a major assembly. If the fault is not found there and then this assembly is built into the final product. If the inspection now finds the fault, a great deal of additional work is required to disassemble the product to replace the faulty component. Costs arising at this stage are reflected in higher cost of manufacture.

If, on the other hand, the fault is not found in the final inspection and the product leaves the factory, yet further costs arise.

The direct costs which will show up are the warranty costs, the cost of product or assembly or component replacement and the labour costs involved. What will not show up are the considerable administrative costs involved in negotiating with the customer, holding spare parts, packing them and getting them to the customer and back again to the factory, re-working these parts and feeding them back into the pipeline. These latter costs are just lost in the evaluation.

What is more, the customer has invested in a new product which, if it breaks down shortly after being taken into service, causes him to be dissatisfied with the supplier. This is never reflected in the supplier's cost but it will show up in the longer term by this customer choosing a different supplier when it comes to reordering, or it will take the salesmen much longer to convince the customer to stay with this supplier.

Many of these costs do not show up in the manufacturing division's management accounts and they were therefore not considered when evaluating the benefits of improving the quality of the product. These cost were being absorbed in general overheads or in higher costs in other divisions. Nevertheless, the company as a whole had to make provisions throughout the other functions involved to cope with the costs which arose due to lack of attention to quality.

Wastage

When competition became tougher and price increases could not just be absorbed and passed on to the customer, companies started to think about improving their product quality primarily driven by a desire to reduce wastage and keep their cost base low. In a study carried out in the U.K. in 1978 it was shown that the total cost of wastage amounted to almost 15% of turnover, costing at that time between £10 billion and £15 billion per year.

This led to improving the information flow between the field and the factory and started the change from simply handling problems that arose in the field into a more thorough management of the underlying issues which caused the problem in the first place. By understanding more fully where the problem originated, enabled companies to take more meaningful remedial actions.

At that time the endeavour was still mainly concerned with reducing wastage rather than improving product quality per se.
The drive to improve product quality for its own sake was forced on industries by Japanese successes. Let us look at the development of Japanese industries since the war and the impact they had on industries in Western countries.

The Japanese Example

Before I even start on this section, let me say right at the beginning that many of the best Western companies have used most of what we now consider to be the Japanese product quality concepts for a long time prior to Japanese companies. There are few, however, who, prior to this decade, developed a total strategy for their companies around quality or who implemented these programmes with the thoroughness and complete dedication shown by most of the Japanese companies that have become household names in the West.

In the immediate post-war years the goods that flooded the world from Japan were considered cheap and shoddy. With their reputation for low quality, the future looked bleak for Japanese goods penetrating Western countries. Japan Inc. then sought the help of two American quality experts, Dr. W. Edward Deming and Dr. J.M. Juran, to assist in improving the quality image of Japanese products. Whereas we, nowadays, talk about the Japanese quality approach, they do not claim authorship of the concept and, even today, the highest award for quality in Japan is still the cherished Deming Prize, named after the American who introduced Statistical Process Control to Japan.

Dr. Deming had realised already before the war that quality could not be inspected into a product but had to be built into it. Being a statistician by training, he developed his approach of studying each component and each procedure employed in the manufacturing process to reduce the variation of quality. This led to a more consistent product. He also taught that by manufacturing up to a quality rather than down to a cost was going to improve profitability in the medium and long term and he asked companies to sacrifice short term profits for medium and longer term benefits.

It was the same message that he had taught during the war years in the United States but his message was not listened to very carefully and implementation of the approach was only patchy, with the consequent lack of positive results.

When he started propagating his message in Japan in the late forties and early fifties, Japanese industrialists listened carefully and implemented what they heard thoroughly by involving all their staff. Quality soon improved, manufacturing processes were redesigned and Japanese products became very competitive on world markets.

This success created an obsession in Japanese companies for producing products of the highest quality and the drive for "Zero Defect" became a real endeavour. This led to the conviction within Japanese companies that they could only succeed if they were "dantotsu", the best of the best.

Statistical Process Control

In aiming for a zero defect, it was necessary to apply Deming's statistical process control in every part of the factory. By ensuring that even small variations in quality are identified enabled companies to take remedial action to improve quality well before it drifted out of standard. It also enables them to identify specific areas, machines or individuals which contributed to the deviation from standards and to find the cause (not symptom) of the problem.

An example often quoted is the manufacturer who found that the name-plate labels were sometimes glued on crookedly. By examining the problem more closely they were able to trace it back to two workers. Instead of simply admonishing them to be more careful, the company found that these two workers were far-sighted and the problem was resolved by providing glasses for the two workers concerned.

The statistical control process starts from the design of the product and not only when it reaches the production floor. Once a company can identify where in the process a defect is likely to occur they can minimise its occurrence.

As many parts and sub-assemblies are not manufactured by the O.E.M. (original equipment manufacturer) himself, it is obviously necessary for him to ensure that the items he is incorporating in his products are of the requisite quality and this has led to many manufacturers insisting that their suppliers also introduce statistical process control methods.

Once the components manufactured within the factory as well as those provided by vendors were of consistently high quality, it was possible to consider different stocking procedures. If the manufacturer can rely on the fact that the components being delivered to the assembly line (from internal and external sources) were all usable, it was no longer necessary to keep large and expensive stocks of components as a buffer between component production and assembly.

This led to the decision to go to "Just In Time" (JIT) stocking procedures which has saved industry substantial amounts not only in the fact that resources (money, space, handling) did not have to be tied up in maintaining large stocks but also in reducing obsolescence.

However, JIT would only work if the user could rely not only on the quality of the product but also on delivery schedules from the supplier which also meant more reliable support services from other (non-production) staff in the manufacturer's own company and in that of the supplier. This was shown to involve every function within the company, as customer requirements could not be met unless all activities were performed correctly and to a predetermined schedule. For instance, it was shown that in many cases the various administrative processes involved in scheduling a production order occupied more time than the manufacturing process itself.

This has led to the development of

Quality Standards

which would give the customer an assurance that the supplier had the systems and procedures to produce high quality products and services. A number of standards or certification schemes exist in the U.K., e.g. BS5750 Parts 1, 2 or 3, (and its equivalent ISO9000), BS4891, BS9000 or PVQAB (Pressure Vessels Quality Assurance Board) etc.

The standard with which we should get familiar in the context of 'Customer Satisfaction through Total Quality' is BS5750. This identifies the basic disciplines amd specifies the procedures and criteria to ensure that a product or service which a company provides meets the customers' requirements.

BS5750 is a Quality Assurance System broken down into three parts:

BS5750 Part 1   is for all but the simplest products
                 if the design is not yet established

BS5750 Part 2   is for all but the simplest products
                 if the design is established

BS5750 Part 3   is only for the simplest products

All three parts require proof of a demonstrable system, a management representative, records, control of inspection, measuring and test equipment, sampling procedures, control of non-conforming material, inspection status, protection and preservation, training and inspection of completed items.

In addition Parts 1 and 2 also require proper procedures to be laid down for purchasing, review of system, work instructions, corrective action, control of documentation and changes, and manufacturing control.

Finally Part 1 also requires design control and planning to be documented and monitored.

One other British standard should be mentioned, namely BS4891, 'A Guide to Quality Assurance' which expands the quality assurance systems outlined in BS5750 into a more complete cost-effective quality management system.

It is not the purpose of this book to guide the readers through the complexities of introducing any of these standards but merely to make them aware of their existence. Detailed publications and help in obtaining certification can be obtained from the British Standards Institute, from the Department of Trade and Industry or from the Institute of Quality Assurance.

BS5750 (ISO9000) is an excellent way to a disciplined approach towards the

Total Quality Concept

Having introduced an efficient quality assurance system the next step of integrating this system with other management systems to enable it to be used as a complete, cost-effective quality management system. It encompasses not only the working processes, disciplines and standards but also the wholehearted cooperation of staff, its involvement and motivation and the recognition that only the best is good enough.

It has become clear that that there is an interdependence between the activities of the various functions within a company and it is difficult for one of them to aspire to zero defects if the support from other areas is not forthcoming at an equally high level.

The users of the output of any person's activity is a "customer", just as surely as the end user is a customer. If each person then regards the user of the output of his work as his customer and treats his requirements with the same concern as he should treat that of an outside customer who pays his wages, each activity will be done as efficiently as possible. This is the basis of total quality – every activity by each member of the staff needs to be performed to an agreed criteria, to the satisfaction of the "customer". In most instances it is a defect in the system or in the process which detracts from providing the necessary output quality.

The concept of an "internal customer" being just as real as a customer who actually pays for a product must become a reality, if Total Quality is to become a way of life within a company.

This is as true in a service industry as it is in a manufacturing industry and very often the same methods of statistical process control can be adapted to the office environment. For instance, customer complaints often arise due to the length of time it takes for the service supplier, be it a bank, an insurance company or any other business, to respond to a telephone call. It can often be established that incoming callers had longer waiting times at certain times of the day or certain days of the week. Once the pattern of the problem is identified, a solution can often be found quite easily.

Having decided that every part of the organisation will have to perform its respective tasks to an agreed quality, the question arises of how to reach the necessary level of commitment in every member of the staff and we will cover this in some depth elsewhere in this book. One other aspect which belongs to "background" is to consider who can most effectively contribute to improving quality. The obvious answer is the people most closely concerned with doing the work. This has led to the formation of

Quality Circles

Quality circles bring together volunteers in a working group on a regular basis to identify and resolve their own work related problems and, with the approval of management, implement solutions in their own work environment.

Obviously these quality circles need to be coordinated and guided to produce optimum results across the company. The crux, however, is to release the knowledge and skills of the work-force to resolve problems in their own work environment as they are likely to be more knowledgeable about their specific job than anyone else. Also, by involving them in resolving their own issues will improve motivation and ensure thorough implementation with a personal interest in the success of the project.

To enable Quality Circles to work effectively, management must stimulate employees to recognise their own capabilities, showing management's trust in the employee by providing adequate information and training the staff to utilise modern problem solving techniques to reach their conclusions. Fully trained "facilitators" are used to provide all necessary support activities and coordinate efforts between various circles.

Quality circles and, in fact, any total quality programme, will only succeed if senior management is seen to support actively the efforts of the staff. The pay-off of well run schemes is substantial.

CHAPTER III

Reasons for Current Drive for Total Quality – Why Now?

Total quality is really such an obvious management goal that the only thing that needs to surprise us that it has not been defined and striven for in the past. What has changed to make it necessary for management to try to implement total quality concepts now throughout their companies? Let us examine these factors under four main headings (see figure 1.).

Figure 1: The changing world

Changes in Markets

In the immediate post-war years there was a general shortage of products and services and the buyer was at a disadvantage when negotiating for better quality of products and services. The seller was in the driving seat and was able to dictate terms to the customer – the seller was almost doing a favour to the purchaser to let him have the product.

Markets were protected by various government restrictions on currencies, customs duties, import licences and other real and artificial obstacles to foreign vendors to sell their wares on the world markets.

As new materials have become available, machinery was modernised and the bottlenecks in providing the needed products and services were gradually disappearing, companies were able to satisfy buyers' purchasing desires. The shortages of manpower turned into surpluses through improved utilisation of equipment and staff, mechanisation and automation and companies were looking to expand their markets. Pressure was exerted on governments to relax some of their restrictive practices and a much freer exchange of goods and services between countries resulted.

European countries realised that they were working at a disadvantage in comparison with American and Japanese competitors due to the many obstacles to trade within Europe itself. Although the market in the Western European countries is very large, it is fragmented and national interests make it difficult to look at Western Europe as one market, as it is possible to do in the United States and in Japan.

This has lead the twelve countries of the European Economic Community to develop a far-reaching harmonisation programme which is being rapidly implemented and is planned for completion by the end of 1992. At this stage it is probable that all the programmes will not be ready for implementation by that time as political as well as economic considerations have to be satisfied. Nevertheless, a large number of the Community's initiatives have already been approved and are being implemented.

This will not only present innumerable new opportunities to businesses of every type in each of the EEC countries but also a threat to their existing "home markets", which will be opened to competition from other EEC companies. Furthermore, it is likely that this increased competition will not only come from companies within the EEC but also from companies outside the Community, who perhaps have been even more active in preparing for the harmonisation within the EEC than companies of the member states.

Some of these companies, particularly those in Japan and the United States, have realised that total quality and customer support is a powerful competitive weapon and have made progress in using this tool through their subsidiaries, dealers and distributors within the Market.

Changes in Technology

Technology has been changing rapidly over the latter half of this century which necessitates even greater emphasis on quality and customer support.

Products and services intended for the same market segment have become more and more similar and companies have to differentiate themselves from their competitors by using non-product related activities. Many buyers find it difficult to appreciate the fine differences in technology in the products offered to them and they therefore take their purchasing decisions based on the total package offered by the various vendors as perceived by the buyer.

As one senior executive of a multi-national corporation put it:

> "If we are to win in this environment, we are going to have to begin playing a much broader keyboard of non-product added value..."

The context in which he referred to "this environment" was when he was talking about competition. This company, incidentally, introduced a Customer Care and Total Quality programme some five years ago and after listing the many financial and commercial benefits the company has gained from it, the same executive stated that after these five years he feels that they are beginning to scratch the surface of the issue.

Another aspect of technological change over the past decades is the move from stand-alone products to a range of products interfacing with one another. This is obviously increasing the pressure on high quality products and support services, as the customer's operational efficiency increasingly depends on the equipment being used and its continuing operation has a direct effect on the productivity of the business.

Let me give you a simple example of what I mean. If, in the past, a bank used 20 typewriters in a particular section of its activity, and one of these typewriters became inoperative, it was an inconvenience for the section but did not have a major effect on its productivity. Now that these typewriters have been replaced by 20 workstations connected to one central processing unit (CPU) and a fault occurs in the CPU, then the effectiveness of the whole section is immediately put in jeopardy and the quality of the support provided by the vendor (or some other supplier of support services) will be a vital part of the decision making process when purchasing a new system.

The increase of data links both on local networks and over distances is again highlighting the need for total quality in the hardware, software and support activities of the supplier.

A third effect of new technologies on total quality and customer care is the much improved facilities for collecting data and organising and planning activities with these management tools. If, by using these tools, a vendor can improve the product or support to customers, the vendor will be able to gain a valuable competitive advantage.

The best known example in this area is the reservation system which was introduced by American Airlines about a decade ago. This airline made a large number of terminals available to some of the largest travel agents (free of charge), which enabled these agents to interface with the airlines reservation system and directly confirm a seat availability to a customer while talking to him. This gave the airline such an important competitive advantage that the authorities considered this to be unfair competition and asked American Airlines either to discontinue the practice or to put flights of other airlines on the same system. The airline decided to go with the second alternative. They still provide the service free to travel agents if the flight is booked on their own airline and make a very small charge for flights booked on competitive airline flights. As a result they still take a major part of the business and they are making a very impressive profit from the small service fee they are charging to the travel agents for booking their clients on other flights.

It does not need to be a large organisation to use these technologies in improving their customer support activities and we will discuss some other examples in chapter XI.

Economic Pressures

With an increased choice of suppliers, companies have found that customers are no longer willing to tolerate manufacturers' or suppliers' inefficiencies and they voted with their wallets. In the "good old days" manufacturers just shrugged off the loss of a customer, knowing full well that they could find others.

This process invariably increased their sales costs, as it is obviously more expensive to keep finding new customers than to retain existing ones. It is estimated that it costs five times as much to gain a new customer as it does to retain an existing one. This extra cost was, in turn, passed on to the customer in higher prices.

At the same time the manufacturing costs were inflated by a high level of returned products or parts which had to be reworked, returned to vendors or scrapped. In addition to the extra direct costs, the cost of administering the flow of products and components, multiple handling and necessary safety stocks to cater for sub-standard parts increased the cost basis of the manufacturer and either made him increase his price or reduce his margin.

Further unnecessary costs were incurred by the field organisation in handling customer complaints, sending field staff to customers to repair faulty products or spend more time during the installation in commissioning them.

Most important of all was the demotivating effect that all these inefficiencies were having on the manufacturer's and the supplier's staff. When staff realises that management does not put any emphasis on efficiency, the natural desire to do a good job vanishes which further reduces the quality level of the product or service provided.

Manufacturers and suppliers therefore found themselves in a squeeze. The customer was demanding better value for money by insisting on high quality of products and support and the manufacturer's costs were rising due to lack of quality of his product or service which was accentuated by disinterested staff.

All this was happening at a time when markets were becoming more open and companies were more exposed to international competition. Even protective actions in many countries could not stem the tide of foreign (initially Japanese and later other Far Eastern) products taking an increasing market share. A number of industries were almost completely taken over by products emanating from these countries because the customer perceived them to be of very high quality and good value for money.

This has lead to the recognition by many companies that drastic changes had to take place to increase customer satisfaction. It was soon recognised that a high quality product was an entry requirement in the competitive race and the race proper would then be fought with other factors of customer satisfaction.

Initially companies felt that improving quality would increase their costs but those who introduced a concerted total quality programme found that the opposite was true. Providing higher quality products and services enabled them to increase their prices (because of the greater value to the customer) and at the same time lowered their costs, as they reduced scrap, unnecessary negotiation with customers, multiple handling and other incidental expenditure. This greater marketing flexibility has made these companies more competitive and improved the level of motivation of their staff.

Behavioural and Social Drivers

As the market-place has moved from a seller's to a buyer's market, competition has invariably increased and the fight for market share has become much tougher. Customers are increasingly searching for better value for the money they are spending (very different from the lowest price) and suppliers who have built a reputation for high quality products and a support organisation willing and able to help the customer are at a clear advantage.

Customers have also become much more knowledgeable about what is available on the market. The publicity of companies themselves and of the media in general is making customers aware of their choices and there has also been an increase in consumer research by specialised bodies and publications which review products in various fields giving the customer a general overview of the features of the product or service, its quality, the speed and effectiveness of handling any issues arising and comparing each parameter with that of the competition and with the price charged.

The customer can thus make his purchasing decision based on broadly researched findings.

With the increased prosperity of many buyers and their desire for more leisure time and better support to their own customers, purchasers are willing to pay for both higher quality and for non-product values provided by the vendor.

As many of the contacts made between the customer and the vendor company are through the vendor's staff, it is important that every member of staff is highly motivated and fully aware that the company is determined to be a winner by providing the customer with a high quality product and excellent support.

A Quality Manager in a large insurance company established that the company's clients found the way their claims were handled of almost equal importance to the claimant as the actual outcome of the issue.

From this we can see that it is not only important to produce a high quality product or provide an excellent service but it is also important to make it known to existing and potential customers that we are doing so – we will discuss this more fully in chapter XIII.

CHAPTER IV

What is Total Quality?

When customers buy a product or service from our company, they do not just consider the product or service in its own right but they look at the total package to decide whether it provides what they require. The needs of the same customer may differ from occasion to occasion.

Let us look, for example, at eating out. On the first occasion a couple plan to go out to celebrate their wedding anniversary and in the second instance they want a fast meal before catching the train home after having spent the early evening at the sales. In both cases they will want a good quality meal in a clean restaurant but the total package will be very different.

In the first case they are likely to want a leisurely meal, in comfortable surroundings, with, perhaps, a little soft music and an attentive waiter willing and able to advise on various dishes and wines, carefully laid tables and they will not wish to rush from one course to the next. In the second instance they are much more likely to be concerned with the speed of the service and the efficiency with which they are served.

It is likely that they will choose different restaurants for each of these occasions because they know that restaurants, like vendors of other products and services, tend to cater for different market segments.

How do customers then make their choice? They are likely to consider both tangible and intangible elements.

Tangible Elements

Tangible elements are factors which can, in some way, be observed and which can usually be measured. That does not mean that customers necessarily apply a measure to the specific parameter but it will, nevertheless, affect their decision.

The quality of the product or service is almost certain to be high up on the list of factors on which customers will make their purchasing decision. But whereas quality is very important, customers find it difficult to measure it directly and they will therefore apply indirect measures and take their decision based on previous experience, the reputation of the manufacturer or supplier and recommendations from trusted people.

The features of the product will also be highly important – obviously it will have to be able to perform the tasks for which the customer is making his acquisition.

Delivery is another essential element in the decision. Many orders have been lost because suppliers have not been able to meet customer delivery requirements or because they have fallen down on promises made to customers. This aspect is becoming more important in recent years as pressure on companies to reduce inventory costs has made customers realise that it is often more cost effective to pay a little more for an item from a supplier on whose delivery they can rely, than to buy on price alone and be forced to hold more stock to counteract the risk of being let down on delivery.

The reaction time, or speed of response, of a vendor is another important tangible element. As customers are increasingly relying on their suppliers for a wide range of support services, they must feel confident that the supplier can be easily reached and will react quickly. This applies to communication of any type, be it by letter, by telephone or a face to face request for information.

Another important factor is the level of support offered by a supplier. In this area manufacturers and suppliers have begun a much more rigorous differentiation by market segment and, in many industries, there has been a change in the method that customer support is provided. This change of method has again been brought about by economic pressure but also by the easier availability of certain customer support and management tools. For instance, in the technical service field many visits to customer sites can now be avoided by more sophisticated diagnostic tools. In the commercial field, many customer issues are being resolved by skilled staff at the end of a telephone with suitable computer assisted aids instead of by repeated visits by salesmen or service engineer to a large number of small customers.

Obviously, the price of the product or service enters the equation. It has been shown, however, that price is often not the decisive factor in the purchasing decision making process. It is often the supplier's own staff, and particularly his sales staff, who believe price to be the most crucial element. It may sometimes hide a lack of other tangible (and intangible) benefits to the customer, which implies that he is not getting value for money rather than that the product is too expensive.

Price is also an easy pretext for a customer to turn away a supplier when he may have taken the decision for other reasons, which might be more awkward to explain to a supplier.

The concept of Total Quality, therefore, starts out by ensuring that the customer really does get tangible benefits from the product or service provided to him, in the area of product and service quality as well as in the total package of tangible and intangible elements provided. Adding value beyond the product or service will enable the supplier to charge a premium price. Naturally, the customer must be made aware that he is getting, or is going to get, these additional benefits so that he realises that he is buying value for money.

Intangible Elements

In many respects, these intangible factors are much more difficult to provide to customers. They involve empathy between the employees of the customer and the supplier and a genuine customer orientation throughout the supplier's organisation. This means that management must influence attitudes of its staff which is a much more difficult and a longer term task than ensuring that the tangible elements are satisfactory.

Human relations are at the core of the issue – human relations both within the supplier's organisation and the relationship with customers. Some of these relationships are a question of skills which can, and must, be imparted to our staff but others are attitudinal issues which can only be influenced by good management practices and leadership.

One of the most important areas where training can have an immediate impact on customer perceptions is in the field of customer handling skills. There are specific ways of dealing with customer issues which will enable the supplier's staff to deal with customers in a helpful and sensitive way. These issues may arise during personal dealings with customers, or on the telephone or in correspondence. Within these areas, the handling of complaints has a special position.

This part of the human relation issue is relatively easy, although it must be realised that one training programme in customer handling skills is unlikely to be sufficient. There is a need for continued on the job training and occasional refresher training. It is much easier for a supervisor to identify a salesman's weakness in selling ability or a service engineer's lack of technical skills than to recognise a need for refresher training on customer handling skills.

On the attitudinal aspect we will spend a little more time in chapter IX. Let me just mention here and now that we cannot expect our staff to service the customer if we do not service our staff. We must put more emphasis on getting our internal human relationships right.

To achieve total quality we will have to have a much greater involvement of our staff in the operational issues of their own areas, and quality circles are one of the ways in which this is being achieved in a number of companies. There are many other ways to ensure this involvement but it is a structured and well documented way of doing so.

It will also mean a consistent approach by management to decision making and to reinforcing their words by relevant actions. Staff must know what to expect from their managers and to be certain of their support when resolving customer issues.

Although it is self-evident that no organisation can exist without satisfying its customers, this fact is certainly not clearly understood all along the line in a company. This lack of understanding is often caused by target setting which does not put customers in the focus – it is aimed at activity rather than result.

These targets are also often conflicting between individual departments in a company which will cause inter-departmental friction and be an obstacle to good team work. As one Chief Executive put it:

"At the heart of the problem is not some villain who consciously ignores the customer. It is a system failure... a leadership failure... and most of all a cultural lapse"

So when it comes to target setting, decision making or any other major decision, we must always put the question: "How will this affect the customer?".

There are other intangible elements which need to be resolved by management and which will result from an attitudinal change within company staff. It is a question of the impression created by an organisation on a customer or a potential customer. Once our staff get sensitised to "Customer Care" some of these issues will resolve themselves and it will become second nature to everyone to "Think Customer". We have, unfortunately, become somewhat insensitive to the image that our company creates in the customer's mind.

Let me just give you a small example. I took one of my clients to one of his suppliers and even before we parked the car my client remarked: "John, this company is not very customer orientated". When I protested that he surely could not tell before we even had gone through the entrance door, he drew my attention to the arrangement of the car park. The spaces nearest the door were reserved for top management of the company (and, incidentally, were largely empty) and the visitor's parking area was some way away. Furthermore, visitors usually stay only a short time at the company and therefore are likely to make more use of the spaces near the door.

Now I am not suggesting that the layout of the company's car park affected this client's decision to a great extent but what I am suggesting is that if there is a cluster of these intangible elements, the customer will be affected, if not consciously, at least subconsciously. Each of these intangible elements in itself may be unimportant, but together they contribute to the image of a company in a customer's mind.

Prevention rather than Detection

Just as in Dr. Deming's approach to product quality, where the drive is to eliminate faults rather than to try to inspect each item at the end of the line to see whether it meets certain standards, there is a need to prevent aspects of our operations which may create an unfavourable image on the customer. This brings me back to the need to examine every decision, every action and every target with a view of its impact on the customer.

At first this will need a conscious effort to examine the impact of every move on the customer. However, with a little experience of using this approach, it will become second nature to every member of the company and, even if the decision itself may not be different, we will have considered its effect on the customer and perhaps be able to present it in a way to indicate that customer needs have not been ignored.

This is of particular importance in the planning stages of products, programmmes or projects because at that time the customer is a long way away from being high on the priority list of the Programme Manager. The prime goals of a Programme Manager are likely to be product costs, time schedule and any necessary trade-off of features. By "Thinking Customer", we will prevent many a problem arising at a later stage which will make it necessary to implement late changes, usually at great cost to the company.

To achieve Total Quality at the customer end requires teamwork all along the supply chain, including ancilliary activities. Every member of the company must be aware of how his or her work impacts the rest of the company's activities. This brings me to the need to identify one's customer.

CHAPTER V

Who is my Customer?

At first sight the answer to this question may seem obvious, but let us look at the question in a little more detail. Let us start with the ultimate user.

The Final User

Our products and services must, naturally, be designed and developed in line with the final user's requirement in mind. This is not quite as easy as it appears when our day to day pressures and priorities may be far removed from the customer. It is easy to forget him when our superior sets us task oriented goals which do not have any apparent relevance to customer requirements.

The inventor or designer may believe that the technological brilliance of an idea is more important than to provide the customer with the features he wants. Or an administrator may think it more important for the customer to conform to the company's ordering procedures than to consider that the customer has also developed his internal systems to which he would like the ordering process to conform. All of us see our own issues much more clearly than those of our customers.

We must never forget that it is the final customer who ultimately pays all our salaries. In the long run customers can do without us but we cannot do without customers.

By bearing in mind these self-evident adages when we take our decision, we could well ensure a greater customer satisfaction and consequent loyalty to our company. The decisions I am referring to do not necessarily affect the product or service that we are providing to our customer directly, they may be internal company issues which affect the customer indirectly. Just think of the arrangement of the car park mentioned in Chapter IV.

It is not that an executive in the company goes out of his way to try and make life more difficult for customers. It is much more likely an omission of a positive customer orientated approach which causes these problems.

This cultural lapse is reinforced by the standard approach to depicting organisational charts. These charts invariably have the Chief Executive at the top of the pyramid and, moving down the pyramid, we find the heads of divisions, the departmental managers, supervisors, and, at the broad base of the pyramid, the workforce, i.e. the designers, the machine operatives, the billing clerks, telephonists, service staff, salesmen, etc. By definition, the next step down, outside the organisation, are "The Customers".

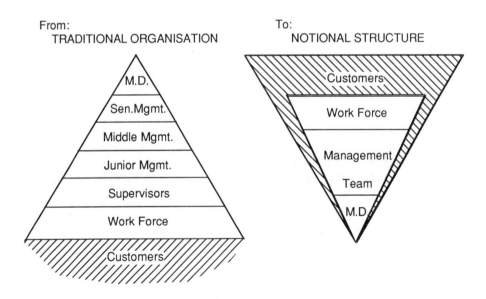

Figure 2: Customers to the top

By creating this model in our minds and in the minds of our staff, it is natural to regard the requirements of our superiors as more important than those of our customers. We as managers are not always very good at ensuring that the goals we set for ourselves and our staff are, in every case, considering the customer as well as the tasks set by our own senior managers.

If we could, conceptually in our minds, reverse the pyramid (see figure 2) and put "The Customers" at the top, with the staff who carry out the real activities within the organisation next to the customers and, as we move up the management ladder, gradually lower on the pyramid to the point at the bottom, we might take more customer oriented decisions. By doing so it is likely that we will improve our customers' satisfaction, raise the morale of our staff, and achieve better results throughout.

By analysing the "raison d'etre" of management we will find that its main purpose is to make the work of those who actually perform the activities throughout the company as effective and efficient as possible, to coordinate their tasks, to plan for the future and direct current activities towards the longer term targets.

In this leadership role, managers must not only state that the "customer is king" but must demonstrate by their actions and decisions that these words are not mere platitudes.

The acid test applied to all decisions within the company should be "How does this affect the final user?".

The Intermediaries

Staff in many companies do not have any (or only very little) contact with the final user. Their products or services are sold through intermediaries who become the direct customer of the producer. Employees in this type of company are often not clear whether their customer is the intermediary company, e.g. a wholesaler, or dealer, or sole agent, or whether the customer is the final user.

In fact they have to regard both as their customers. The only way they can reach the final user is through the intermediary and they must, therefore, be able to satisfy the intermediary's requirements. If the product or service, however, does not comply to the needs of the final user, it will be very difficult for the intermediary to sell it.

Selling through an intermediary is thus more difficult, as we have to satisfy the needs of both the dealer and the final user. One effective way to make it more attractive for the dealer to do business with us is for us to remember the purpose of any company – to make profits for itself by satisfying customer needs. This applies even more strongly to the dealers (who tend to take a very short-term view) than to the manufacturers.

The usual pressure from dealers to increase their profits is to ask the manufacturer for a higher discount (or a lower price) which, of course, will affect either the manufacturer's margins or the selling price to the final user, which in turn may adversely affect volume. There is another way the manufacturer can deal with this issue.

As the dealer's profit is made up of the difference between the buying and selling price less his own expenses, his profits can be increased by lowering his expenses. By making it easy to deal with us, by training his staff, providing all relevant information and documentation in an easily absorbable form and showing a genuine interest to help him provide an outstanding service to his customers, we will lower his costs, increase his profits and motivate him to sell our products instead of those of the competition.

Let me give you a couple of examples. Early in my career I worked for a machine tool company who, in addition to making a small range of machine tools themselves, were distributors of a wide range of American machine tools throughout Europe. Some of our principals gave us limited support, hardly ever visited us or our customers (the users), and it was difficult to extract information from them. Others ensured that we were visited by their experts on a regular basis, these experts made visits to customers with us which benefited the customers and was a great learning experience for us. They provided us with all necessary support, delivered as per promises and we developed a mutual respect for one another. This reduced my employer's costs, motivated us (the staff) and demonstrated to the user that we, (the dealer), as well as the manufacturer had a genuine interest in him. Obviously, this approach to the intermediary gave benefits to everyone – the manufacturer (more business and first-hand feedback), the dealer (more profit) and the end user (better support).

Another example from more recent times. One of my clients is making terminals available to his major distributors free of charge to interface direct with his order entry system which enables them to get up to the minute delivery data, simplifies their ordering procedure and reduces both parties' administrative costs. Not surprisingly, this client's business with these distributors increased considerably more rapidly than with others. The client drew the obvious conclusion and is expanding the facility to a larger number of distributors.

These are just two of innumerable examples which can be quoted indicating that intermediaries will respond to positive action by the supplier to assist them in improving their profits without adversely affecting the margins of the manufacturer.

In all cases both the manufacturer and the distributor are hoping for a long term relationship and are willing to work closely together to provide a better support to the ultimate customer for the benefit of all concerned.

Clearly the manufacturer has identified that he has two customers, the dealer and the end user.

Internal Customers

Business and industry are becoming increasingly more complex and the people in direct contact with the customer are less and less able to satisfy the final user's needs without the support of everyone else in the company. The salesman cannot fulfil his delivery promise to the customer, if the dispatch department does not do their part of the task and they, in turn, have to rely on manufacturing making the product available to them at the pre-arranged time. Manufacturing has to rely on their sub-contractors for quality and delivery and on their own assembly workers, on production engineering staff, designers, etc. It is also important for the customer that his supplier continues in business, as he wants to buy from him in the future as well, and therefore the goods have to be invoiced, the money collected to assure adequate cash flow, and support provided from other company functions.

The modern way of looking at any user of the output of our work is to regard him as a customer, be he inside the company or outside. If we genuinely regard the user of our work as "OUR" customer, establish jointly how this output can be made most useful to him and arrange suitable measures to monitor performance, then Total Quality is assured.

It is much easier, of course, to identify the internal user of our work and his specific requirements than it is to do so with final users. Yet, many companies spend large sums in researching customer needs (see next Chapter) without encouraging employees of different departments in the same company to get together and establish the requirements of the internal customer.

This is more than merely a conceptual change; it will affect the whole way in which company targets are agreed and fulfilled, it has organisational implications and demands greater team work between various functions in a company. It is no longer sufficient to "Maximise" the goals of an individual function, as this maximisation in one function's goals may sub-optimise the results of the whole company.

By regarding the user of the output of our function as our customer and by utilising the "Acid Test" mentioned earlier, of questioning how our decisions will affect our customer, we will ensure that our company's results are optimised; this may mean internal trade-offs between functions. This implies greater involvement between various functions and a total company approach.

These changes have been instrumental in flattening the company's management pyramid from a largely hierarchical structure to a project or task orientated organisation.

By satisfying our immediate customer's needs and continually keeping an eye on the final user's requirements, we are going to achieve Total Quality throughout our organisation.

CHAPTER VI

Establishing Customer Needs

Establishing the needs of an internal customer should be relatively easy, provided management create the right environment and attitudes for employees at all levels to work together for the common goal. Provided the company culture and environment have created a team approach it should not be too difficult to establish the internal customer's needs and to agree specific standards by a planned communication process.

In practice it is often found that there is a great deal of internal company friction, politicking and buck passing caused by conflicting goals and measures which we will discuss later (Chapter VIII).

Here we will concentrate on the issues arising from trying to establish external customers' needs.

The Identification Process

The approach to identifying customer needs will, of course, differ from industry to industry depending on the type of product, the number and location of customers and the company's mission. For instance, if we are producing oil drilling rigs, we have a limited number of potential customers and our approach to establishing customer needs will be different to a mass produced item or a company in the service industry such as banking or insurance.

We will discuss various methods of establishing customers' requirements and each manager will have to select the approach most suitable to the conditions prevailing in his industry. In all cases, however, the emphasis must be on what the customer perceives to be his needs and how he perceives your company in comparison to your competitors, rather than by your own internal measures.

This does not mean that you do not have to have your own internal criteria to help you achieve customer perceived requirements, but what it does mean is that your internal measures should be oriented to meet the needs as perceived by the customer. If, for instance, your customers do not perceive delivery within two days instead of within four days to be a benefit, it is likely to be an unnecessarily expensive exercise for you to set a two day target.

Obviously, therefore, it is necessary to have good communication with your customers and here are a few ways this is being done:

The most direct and interactive method is to obtain and evaluate the feedback from your own staff who are in contact with the customer (e.g. sales staff, service staff, etc). To ensure that this useful source of information is not lost, it is necessary for management to institute simple procedures which consume little time for your field staff to feed back information from the customer. It is also essential to demonstrate to your staff that this information is actively used to take customer orientated decisions because, if the information loop is not closed, the flow of information will dry up.

The disadvantage of this approach is that the information may be filtered by the staff concerned and may not accurately represent the customers' opinions. We should bear in mind, however, that our staff who are in most direct contact with customers are more likely to be able to contribute to helping us to establish customers' genuine needs than other staff.

The next most direct approach is to have a formalised survey of customers or of a selection of customers. This can be done by telephone or with a well designed questionnaire. Customers are increasingly willing to communicate with their suppliers about their feelings of the support they are receiving, particularly once they realise that the answers given are seriously evaluated. It is usually good practice to inform customers which of their suggestions will be pursued and which, for justifiable reasons, cannot be pursued. Some suppliers have developed a system of approaching all their customers in turn, say a quarter of the customers every three months and, after employing this approach for a number of years, they are getting a very high percentage of responses.

It is just as important and, perhaps, even more useful to establish why former customers are no longer buying the company's products or services. Many customers do not complain when they have a problem and just vote with their feet by not continuing to give their business to the company. Establishing what part of our activities have not been found satisfactory to these ex-customers can often highlight areas where a company must take remedial action.

Some companies feel that customers will be reluctant to provide honest responses to difficult questions if these questions are put by the company themselves. In these circumstances outside market research organisations are often employed to identify customer attitudes to the company.

If independent market research companies are employed to evaluate customer opinions, it is usual to get them to establish customer relative perceptions not only of the company's own products and/or services but also those of their competitors. This will enable the company to establish bench-marks for the best performers in individual fields of customer requirements and to measure themselves against those bench-marks. We will come back to this subject later when we talk about standards in Chapter VIII.

It is very usual to make use of a number of approaches together to ensure both a general comparative understanding of customer requirements through a market research study as well as an individual customer orientated direct survey.

Another widely used way of establishing customer needs is a customer audit or a visit of customer executives to our company. A customer audit consists of a number of supplier's executives arranging a visit to the customer to review past performance and to discuss how both companies could benefit in the future by closer cooperation. These audits frequently start by the customer raising problems which have occurred in the past and which have, hopefully, been resolved some time ago but after this "letting off steam" the discussion usually becomes very constructive and the supplier can often understand the customer's issues more clearly and ensure appropriate action.

In the opposite situation, where customer's executives visit the supplier, a positive atmosphere is often established by the visiting V.I.P's. being shown some interesting part of the supplier's activity. This may be a visit to the factory, or the demonstration of a new order handling system which speeds the customer's orders through the supplier's procedures, or some other new development such as a new warehousing approach or an automated dispatch of service staff to the customer. After that, executives from the customer and from the supplier sit down together to talk about future developments on both sides.

Many companies also encourage and organise customer user groups which enable customers from different firms to meet together and exchange experiences. Some companies are reluctant to encourage user groups as they feel that these groups will develop into pressure groups on the supplier. Personally I believe that customers will have discussions in any case, be it in trade association meetings, exhibitions or elsewhere and it must be beneficial to the supplier if he can be there to hear first-hand what customers have to say and to be able to correct any misconceptions which may have arisen.

One of the most neglected sources (until the last few years) for establishing customer needs and attitudes are complaints. In the past individual customer complaints were handled and, hopefully, resolved in a positive way and that was the end of the matter. More recently this part of handling of complaints has become only the first step in a complete complaint management procedure. This complaint management approach is an integral part in moving towards Total Quality. It involves careful evaluation of how the customer's dissatisfaction was created and, if appropriate, to change internal procedures to ensure that the same problem does not arise with the same customer or other clients.

In all the above mentioned approaches there is one essential prerequisite. We must genuinely listen to what the customer tells us. This is not as self-evident a statement as it might seem. Listening is a

44

difficult skill – we may hear the words that have been spoken (or written) without trying to understand their full implications and taking on board the message they are trying to convey.

We all think that we are good listeners. In a course on "Listening" which I attended some years ago, it only took some 20 minutes to prove to me that not a single member of our group had really listened properly. All our listening is influenced by our past experiences, by our expectations on the subject concerned and about our opinion of the person delivering the message. The results in the "Listening Course" were obtained in a relaxed attitude where none of the participants had any vested interest.

You can imagine how much more our understanding of what a customer is saying is being influenced under the much more stressful conditions applying in the customer-supplier situation where both parties have their own preconceived ideas and vested interests.

Quantification

Once we have established customer needs we have to find ways of quantifying some of these requirements. On some matters of quantification customers may be quite specific. For instance, when it comes to delivery time of a product, customers are likely to know fairly precisely what they need. For other needs customers may not be as specific. He may wish his equipment to be repaired "as soon as possible", but how fast is "as soon as possible?"

This is where the supplier may have to make some decisions about quantifying specific aspects of customer requirements. Certain attributes which might be desirable for the customer may be quite costly to implement and then it is a question of balancing the cost to benefit ratio for the supplier or the customer. How much more is the customer willing to pay for an improved support activity or will the benefit of additional business from this and other customers more than compensate the supplier for the expenditure?

Not every improvement involves higher expenditure. In fact the achievement of Total Quality is likely to reduce the supplier's total cost in addition to increasing customers' satisfaction. Doing things right the first time reduces the cost of putting them right later on and, at the same time, saving administrative costs and a great deal of aggravation all round.

The danger for suppliers is that they might set themselves targets for improvement which are of limited or no benefit to the customer. Many of these improvements are completely transparent to the customer and he does not even realise that they have occurred. Often consistency is more important to a customer than an improved "average". Let us use an example to illustrate the point:

Customers may have indicated in surveys that response time is important to them when requesting service to their product. (Response time is the time from when the customer notifies a supplier that he requires service until the time that the supplier's service engineer arrives on customer's premises). If the service supplier reduces response time beyond a certain point, the cost of providing the reduced response time rises very rapidly (see figure 3.). From the customer's point of view he may not perceive a difference between an

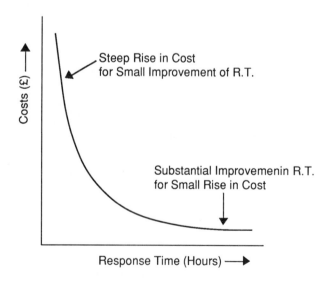

Figure 3: Costs versus response time (R.T.)

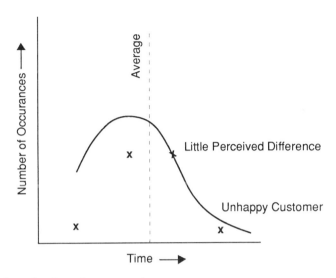

Figure 4: Distribution of response time

average response time of three hours and one of two hours, yet the increase in costs to the supplier would be substantial. What is more important to the customer is the distribution of response times around the average (see figure 4.), i.e. how the three hour average is made up. If it means that sometimes he gets a one hour response time and at others a six or seven hour response time, then the consistency of response time (i.e. the distribution of response time around the average) is more important than the absolute figure of the average. This distribution of response time can be achieved by methods which do not incur a great deal of additional costs but reducing the average is likely to require greater resources.

In consequence it is necessary to clearly understand what the customer means before we take expensive decisions which will give us and the customer limited or no benefits. This brings us to our next subject:

Interpreting Data and Deciding on Actions

Having established customer needs it is now necessary to interpret the raw data. Whereas it is very often necessary to employ a professional market research specialist to devise the methods and wording of a survey questionnaire so as not to obtain the answers that management expects (rather than the customers' unguided opinion), it is usually essential for the company's own staff to interpret the data and develop an action programme.

There was an example of a survey report showing that 20% of potential customers would buy that company's products in preference to that of a competitor, 65% were neutral and had no preference and the remaining 15% would choose the competitors' products in preference to the company's. The first interpretation of this data was that no specific action was required, because only 15% of customers would actively try and buy a competitor's products. The interpretation that was subsequently put on the data was that 80% of the customers would not choose the company's products in preference to that of competitors and they therefore instituted a Customer Satisfaction and Total Quality programme throughout their organisation and positively influenced their market position.

It is often necessary to get a small group of customers together to probe in depth what a specific positive or negative comment really infers. These in depth workshops need to find the underlying cause of the comment rather than merely the effect. In an internal company attitude survey of their own staff a particular action caused a great deal of adverse comment. By conducting an in depth workshop with a limited number of staff it transpired that it was not the action itself which caused the dissatisfaction but the additional use that was made by management of the data provided.

A once-off survey may be of little benefit to a company. What will be much more important is to follow trends and see how specific actions affect these trends.

Collecting and analysing data has no purpose in itself unless we actively use the information we have obtained. I am often surprised at the wealth of information that is available in a company's data bank which is not made available to staff who could put it to good use which would assist them in making better, and more customer oriented, decisions.

In consequence we need to establish carefully what the customer requirements really are, to quantify in a meaningful way how these requirements could be met and to make sure that the information is interpreted from the customer's point of view. The most important part remains: deciding on appropriate action to be taken (or not to be taken) from the results obtained.

CHAPTER VII

Satisfying Customer Needs Profitably

Having established customer needs and having interpreted the data it is essential to understand

The Costing Process

As was touched upon in the last chapter, some of the actions which a company may wish to implement will have a front-end cost which will take some time to recover. Others will simply mean improving internal procedures and methods which will, in fact, save costs even in the short term.

Do not shy away from those projects which may mean initial investments which, in some instances, may be quite considerable. Most projects will involve development and training costs which are part of the educational expenditure. Others may involve relatively high investments in capital expenditure to utilise (and develop) modern management tools to run a more efficient operation and these will be discussed in detail in chapter XI.

It will not be very difficult to persuade top management to proceed with projects which will not only improve customer satisfaction but which will, at the same time, reduce the costs incurred, e.g. by reducing the amount of rejects or speeding up the collection of outstanding debts. Frequently the reason for not having changed inefficient methods and processes is lethargy and an inward focus in a company. It will take considerable skills of persuasion to convince top management to change the inward, process oriented, outlook to an outlook which focusses on the customer, particularly if it will also require expenditure for projects which involve substantial front-end investment.

It is often not a question that top management is averse to investments in projects designed to improve customer satisfaction provided it is convinced that there will be a benefit in the medium or longer term. Frequently operational managers dare not ask for these investments, as they are not able to effectively justify the expenditure (lack of financial know-how) or their fear that the proposal may highlight weaknesses within their area of responsibility. In the financial evaluation of these projects operating managers often find it much easier to establish the costs of a project than to commit to financial benefits. If operating managers are unwilling to commit to achieving a benefit they cannot blame top management for their reluctance to support the scheme.

The reason why managers are usually conservative in their estimates of the benefits is that they know that they will be expected to achieve the forecast results and they cannot be certain that their estimates are realistic. There is, therefore, a tendency to opt for under-estimating the benefit so as to make it relatively easy to achieve it.

From many years of personal experience as an operational manager and, more recently, as a consultant to other companies I have found that benefits in customer satisfaction orientated projects tend to be greater than initially envisaged. Very often there are not only the direct benefits which were included in the evaluation of the project but additional ones appear as the customer perceives the benefit and is more willing to do business with us. As customer satisfaction increases, our own staff are motivated by the customer's satisfaction and by working for a customer oriented company and their motivation will be reflected in better support to the customer.

It will also be helpful to identify why we want to follow a particular course of action. Is it defensive (the customer is dissatisfied with what we are providing), is it reactive (a competitor is taking a lead), is it to secure market share (growth) or is it to improve profits. By establishing the strategic purpose of a desired investment it will make it easier for us to justify it to top management.

The common language of all functions within a company is money. Functional managers will have to learn to express their proposals for change in financial terms to get top management to accept their proposals. This will mean quantifying the benefits that will be achieved by the action recommended. This may be fairly easy when we talk about direct product (or service) related actions, such as reducing wastage, an improved inventory system for stock-holding, or a simpler design which will reduce manufacturing costs.

But how do we quantify

The Benefits of Non-Product "Value Added" Service?

In this instance there will be a need to make certain assumptions but these assumptions should be supported with as much data as possible. Here we will have to make use of the information established in our investigation of customer needs (see Chapter VI). We may be able to use information obtained by other departments for different purposes or it may require specific studies.

For instance, if we find that delivery delays are the cause of a large percentage of customers having decided to buy elsewhere and we have developed a scheme by which delivery could be safeguarded in a much larger number of instances, then we must make an assumption how many of these customers we would have retained if we had not had long delivery delays.

It will be more difficult to establish how many additional customers we could have secured if we could ensure more rapid delivery. One way is to make a trial in a limited geographical area against a control area. This is not always easy to do and obviously delays full implementation. On the other hand it will give us more confidence that the project is worth introducing.

Many companies have also found that their existing customers often use more than one supplier for the same product as insurance. This is obviously inconvenient for the customer as he has multiple administrative costs and probably a variation in quality, even though both suppliers deliver within specification. Despite this, customers accept these disadvantages as they are concerned that one or other of their suppliers will not conform to their delivery promises. If our company could guarantee delivery, customers may be willing to place all their business for this product with us, giving both partners benefits. How much is this worth to us? Again, we will have to make certain assumptions.

It is the general trend in these times of Total Quality for customers and suppliers to get closer together, exchange more information and rely on each other to a greater extent. Customers place more business with a more limited number of qualified suppliers. We will discuss this issue more fully in Chapter XII.

Improved services which increase the added value offered to customers often entail a change of process within the supplier and a willingness to review past systems and procedures. It does help to look at the whole process and not to view the situation in a functionally compartmentalised way.

One of my clients, a major chemical company, was able to cut the time between the customer placing an order and receipt of the goods by more than half by introducing a system which combined order entry, credit control, inventory management, packing list, dispatch note and invoicing. In addition to reducing the company's administrative costs, customer satisfaction and confidence in the supplier were increased and this enabled the company to negotiate bulk contracts which further simplified the customer's and supplier's administration and, at the same time, made production planning easier.

It is also important for the supplier to make these benefits known to the customer. Let me give you another example, this time from the computer industry.

A very large customer used an extensive range of computers from two manufacturers. A fire in the computer area damaged a similar range of computers from both suppliers and both manufacturers were immediately alerted. The smaller maker sent in a team of engineers and they got the customer up and working on their computers within three days. The larger manufacturer sent in a team consisting of very senior managers as well as a group of engineers, and whilst the engineers were working on the machines, the senior managers kept in touch with the customer's senior management informing them of progress on a continual basis. The larger manufacturer completed the work in five days. The customer publicly praised the larger manufacturer for his support which gave the company a great deal of publicity. Clearly the smaller manufacturer did a better job in supporting the customer, but the larger company got more credit because they communicated more effectively with the customer's senior management.

The lesson we should learn from this is that it is not good enough to give the customer satisfaction, it is also necessary to make him aware of the benefit he gets by working with us. The customer's perception becomes the reality in his mind.

It demonstrates the positive attitude of both supplier companies in helping the customer in a very efficient way but in the case of the larger company there was, in addition, the understanding that we should be proud of our achievements and not assume that the results achieved will be known throughout the customer's company.

Another benefit which we gain by providing a total quality support to our customers is the feeling of pride it generates within our own staff; all of us want to work for a customer oriented company, to provide high quality of support and to have satisfied customers. All this is highly motivating (see chapter IX).

The range of activities which will add to the customer's perception of a supplier's quality of product and support is limited purely by the creative thinking of the supplier. Many companies provide support which the customer does not even know he would require. There is also the whole cluster of impressions created by company staff, facilities, and image which will influence customers' purchasing decisions.

As pointed out earlier, customers have great difficulty in differentiating between the features of competitive products; this has made the non-product "value added" the crucial area on which companies will increasingly compete to be the preferred suppliers.

There is another area which needs to be considered in this context:

Value versus Price

Although I do not dispute the importance of the price which is charged to a customer, customers are often willing to pay a slight premium if they can rely on the total support provided by the supplier. The perceived value received by the customer is worth a certain differential.

The customer is not particularly interested in our product or service for its own sake – what he is interested in is what the product or service does for him. It is not the intrinsic value that he is buying but the benefit that it will provide for him.

If we can, therefore, give him a product or service which is not only of high quality but where all other aspects of his dealing with us is to his complete satisfaction, the value to him is beyond that of the product itself.

When a customer buys one of our products he is buying all the other support activities that we provide with it. As Tom Peters put it:

> "The essence of excellence is the thousand concrete, minute actions performed by everyone in an organisation to keep a company on course"

The premium a customer is willing to pay will depend on the perceived benefit in dealing with us as compared to our competitors. We can consider this premium like an insurance policy – the customer buys peace of mind in addition to the product.

It has been shown that in many instances the greatest resistance to price tends to come from the company's own employees, and particularly from the sales force. It is, therefore, essential to establish the real source of price resistance, as it may be an internal company issue rather than coming from the customer.

Although price remains an important factor in the customer's purchasing decision, it is seldom the only consideration which will affect the choice of supplier.

Quality has become so important to customers that shoddy goods are no longer acceptable. The new relationship between suppliers and customers, which is being increasingly applied by the best companies thoughout the world, aims to work as a partnership, so that any benefits of saved costs through higher total quality are shared between the supplier and the customer.

CHAPTER VIII

Setting Standards

Although the attitude of a company's staff and management towards customers is the crucial change which must be achieved, we must accept that only if all company staff know precisely what the company's goals are, are we likely to be able to provide a high quality and consistent customer support. These company goals must then be broken down to standards for individual tasks to ensure that everyone has the same understanding. Vague statements such as "As soon as possible" are meaningless as this may mean five minutes to one person and five hours to the next.

In consequence we need specific measures. Some activities cannot be measured directly and these must then be measured indirectly. In most instances it is the customer's perception which will determine whether the standard is satisfactory to him or not and this perception is based not only on his real needs but is also influenced by his expectations. This is yet another reason why everyone in the company must be aware what standards we are currently achieving, as it would be counter-productive for a salesman, for instance, promising a delivery within, say, three days, if the company's standard is five days and the current average seven days.

Direct and Indirect Measures

We have established the customers' needs (Chapter VI) and on each of the parameters identified we should agree clear standards which we intend to achieve.

One of the widely used approaches is to establish for each parameter what our competitors are providing. It is unlikely that the same company is going to provide the best support in every area and it will also not necessarily be appropriate for our company to be "the best" in every one of the factors. However, with this approach the provider of the highest standard is used as a bench-mark against which our own current performance and future goals are compared.

This is where we have to come back to our company's mission statement and from this we deduce to what standards the various activities we undertake should be performed. If this desired standard is very far from our current performance, it is usually necessary to reach the final goal in stages. It will not be motivating to the staff if the targets agreed are unachievable and a step by step approach is recommended.

In the process of agreeing a standard it is highly beneficial if the employees actually performing the tasks in question are involved from an early stage. All of us prefer to produce satisfactory work (we'll talk about this in more detail in the next chapter) and get no pleasure if we ourselves realise that the task has not been performed well and efficiently. Also we must not forget that the people most closely involved with performing a task are more likely to know every detail of the task and therefore are in an ideal position to suggest ways of improving the way it is done. What we, as managers, have to do is to release this desire to perform well and to harness their knowledge and experience.

There are a number of ways in which this can be done, including Quality Circles, Suggestion Schemes, Brainstorming Sessions, etc. The crucial aspect of whatever method is chosen is for management to genuinely listen to their staff and to react (communicate) to what they have heard.

Let us look now at just a few of the areas where standards can, and should, be set. Obviously these will vary from industry to industry and according to the individual company's aims.

Quality of Product or Service:

This is likely to be the most important customer requirement and is likely to be a prerequisite to achieving customer satisfaction. For internal measurement, this has to be broken down into the various stages of the process producing the product or service provided by our company. In the area of product quality a great deal of work has been done and the statistical process control approach is widely used. As with every other standard, however, we have to be very specific as otherwise various members of our staff will have a different understanding of vague statements. Typically it is easier to set standards for product quality than it is to set standards for a company in the service industry.

Quality standards in a manufacturing industry can be directly related to the product as supplied to the customer. In a service industry many of the standards may have to be indirectly measured as the product is not tangible and the "product" is "manufactured" and "used" at one and the same time. These indirect measures can be determined by finding out from customers what aspects of the service are important to him. Let us take a bank as an example.

A customer who wants to withdraw money from his account or pay it in, may judge his bank by the length of time he has to wait before being able to reach the till, the friendliness of the staff, the convenience of opening hours, the surroundings and atmosphere of the bank while he is waiting, as well as on the more direct "product" aspects such as whether his current account pays reasonable interest and the type of restrictions imposed. This brings us into the whole area of support which is an integral part of Total Quality.

Delivery Time:

There are a number aspects of delivery we need to consider. The first is the actual time of delivery and how it compares with the expected (promised) delivery time. Secondly, the consistency of delivery time from one occasion to the other is of prime importance, to enable the customer to plan his own operation efficiently. Thirdly, he will be interested to know how your company can deal with unusual requirements, e.g. where he has had an exceptional demand for some product (unplanned) – in other words the flexibility of your organisation to bypass the usual approach (we will come back to this in the next section). He will also be interested to know how closely you adhere to the stated conditions, i.e. giving the customer an earlier delivery than agreed may be almost as inconvenient to him as being late, as he may not have the necessary storage facilities or manpower available at the unexpected time.

All this is of even greater importance as companies are reducing their stock levels to an absolute minimum as they are moving to a Just In Time (JIT) inventory planning approach. They are finding it more efficient to pay, perhaps, a little more to a supplier on whom they can rely to keep his delivery promises (and, of course, provide high quality products) and thus avoid unnecessary stock levels, reduce multiple handling and administration as well as safeguard against obsolescence.

It will be obvious that delivery is not only the responsibility of the supplier's warehousing and distribution staff. It is a good example of internal customers (discussed in some detail in Chapter V) determining the visible delivery to the customer. The order processing department has to prepare the paper work in time, the factory and all its sub-contractors and work stations have to produce the product, it has to be suitably packaged and prepared for dispatch before the customer can experience delivery on time.

The same importance applies to delivery of a service product. I don't know how many people share my dislike of restaurants where I may go for a meal with a friend and they serve the hot dish to one of us before they bring the other's cold dish. Or where the vegetables intended to be eaten with the main dish arrive when the main dish has been almost eaten or got cold while waiting for "delivery" of the vegetables. The same applies to after-sales service, where some companies pride themselves in fast response time (see next sub-heading) but do not make adequate spare parts available to repair the fault.

Dissatisfaction with delivery time is the cause of very many customers seeking alternative suppliers. If we then calculate how much it costs to secure a new customer to replace the one who has moved to our competitor, it will be apparent that this is an area requiring a great deal of attention by management to satisfy customer needs without increasing their own costs excessively. In many cases a clear understanding of standards throughout the organisation will enable the end user's needs to be satisfied.

Speed of Response:

In addition to the actual delivery time of a product or service we, as customers, are often very sensitive to response time, i.e. the time between first indicating our interest in the product or service (by walking into a shop, or telephoning or writing to a supplier) and the time it takes for someone to take some notice of us.

Many people get very irritated when they walk into a shop, see a number of shop assistants talking to each other and ignoring the customer. This may well build up resistance to making their purchase in that shop. All of us find it irksome to have to wait for minutes at a time before a telephone is answered. One of the serious complaints against the National Health Service in many parts of the U.K. is the waiting necessary before seeing a doctor or receiving treatment.

Being aware that this is an issue is one thing but what can managers do about it? This is where we come into the area of setting standards and measuring performance. Let us take the telephone response time mentioned above as an example. The manager needs to establish how long customers should have to wait before the telephone is answered. This is where averages may be of little use as it will be found that in many companies there are peaks and troughs in the number of telephone calls made or received. It will be the customers who ring during the peak who will encounter excessive waiting times.

In consequence, it will be necessary to log the length of time customers have to wait before the telephone is replied to at different times of the day. This type of equipment is readily available and the number of rings before the 'phone is answered is recorded together with the length of time each call took. This is plotted by quarter hours and over time a pattern is established. Once we have the basic information to hand, managers can take necessary decisions. For instance, in one company it was found that the peak of customer calls was on a Monday morning which coincided with the least availability of staff. By simply reorganising working patterns it was possible to control the waiting time for responding to customers' calls.

The actions taken included ensuring that meetings were not scheduled for Monday mornings, training of less than one week's duration did not start on Monday mornings, own staff were discouraged to telephone during those periods, additional staff were drafted into the telephone answering area, etc. It was impossible for management to take reasonable action until they knew the pattern of telephone activities.

They were then able to agree reasonable standards with their staff. In this instance they agreed to aim for an average waiting time for customers to be only three rings of the telephone and a maximum of five rings. You will note that the standard set covered not only the average but also a maximum. As we pointed out before, customers are only interested in what is happening to them and not in any average for the whole company. (See Chapter VI).

Other improvements suggested by staff included modernisation of the telephone equipment, greater flexibility in working hours and other work aids which enabled the company to achieve their targets without increasing staff.

It is often found that customers are more critical of response time for services rendered by suppliers than they are of total down time. This may be illogical, as the utility to the customer is dependent on down time, of which response time is only one of the factors. Nevertheless, the very fact that the customer is aware that some action is in hand is soothing his nerves. Some companies have, therefore, instituted procedures which keep customers continually informed of what is happening.

Let me give you just two examples. A mail order company supplying a wide range of products has instituted a procedure where the operator dealing with the customer talks him through what is happening. The operator may, for instance, say to the customer: "I am now feeding your requirement into the system, it will take a few seconds to get the item onto the screen and to establish whether it is in stock, here we are, yes, it is in stock...". This gives the customer the feeling that something is happening all the time rather than be put on hold while the operator identifies the status of the product.

Another example is the after-sales service division of a company who have instituted a procedure, where the Service Engineer who is going to deal with the breakdown is immediately notified and is instructed to telephone the customer and discuss the issue with him. Knowing that the Service Engineer is involved tends to make the customer more tolerant to necessary delays and it may also be possible for the engineer to establish the urgency of the issue and the likely cause of the problem, which may enable him to have the right spare parts with him when he actually visits the customer.

Both examples show that, in addition to providing a service to the customer, the two companies in question recognised that the customer appreciates the manner in which that service is provided.

Level of Support:

As in other aspects of Customer Service, when we come to considering the level of support we are going to provide, we must be absolutely clear what market segment we are aiming for. The genuine customer requirements will differ for each segment and, in some cases, even between various times of the day, week or year.

Let us look at the last point raised first. To be really able to support one's customers adequately, the support organisation must know not only the customer's application but also his pattern of work. An after-sales service department which was supporting a major installation in the Universities Clearing House were able to provide the customer with a priority level of support during the six weeks of peak activity of the installation, when most of the prime activity took place, whilst for the rest of the year a normal level of support was adequate.

There are many seasonal activities where customer needs for support may require variable levels – another typical example is the work of Accountants, which peaks around the end of the financial year. Companies who can cater for this variable demand for support will have an advantage over those who have only a fixed level, which may be inadequate during some parts of the year and may be excessively high and expensive at others.

The conclusion this leads to is the need for companies to be able to understand their customer requirements thoroughly, to have the ability to set the level of support they plan to provide and to control and measure its achievement. Obviously it will also be necessary to establish the additional cost involved in providing a higher level of service. It may be possible to employ management techniques to balance workloads and activities so that the better support does not, necessarily, increase costs.

This requires understanding staff, knowledgeable management and the provision of management tools to ensure that the agreed standards are met. Flexibility of approach to customers will create a positive environment in which to do business.

The reason we have taken the customer with variable requirements first is because it is the most difficult situation. Once we are able to cope with this customer's requirements it will be easy to cater for clients with an even workload. As in most other activities, we will have to start with the company's mission and strategy, and from this develop the level of support our organisation wants to achieve. It would be unreasonable to plan to support a portable typewriter to the same level as, say, an aircraft engine. The penalty cost of a failure is much greater to the user of an aircraft engine and he will, therefore, require a higher level of support and be willing to pay for it.

In this connection there is one approach which customers tend to resent. I have sometimes heard a Service Engineer tell a customer: "You only use your equipment 10% of the time so the repair is not so urgent". To the customer the absence of the equipment at the time when he does want to use it is as important as to another, who uses it more fully. I have also heard an Engineer tell a customer: "You have another one of these equipments on the next floor, so your need is not as urgent as some other customer". Understandably the customer replied that he bought two because he needed two and not to allow the company to move his requests for support to the end of the queue.

The only way to achieve a consistent level of support is to set relevant standards as otherwise we cannot adequately communicate with our own staff or with our customers. Wherever possible these standards should be clearly quantified. It is not always possible to set goals which are directly quantifiable and in those cases indirect measures must be employed.

Indirect measures for customer satisfaction with level of support may be the number of customers ordering competitive products or the number of complaints received. The target set is then measured as, for instance, "Reduce the percentage of customers buying competitive products by 'X%' in year one and 'X+Y%' in year two". This overall target must then be broken down into specific support goals.

Indirect measurement can also be applied to issues which, at first sight, seem impossible to quantify. A large manufacturer of office equipment produced a wide range of copiers, duplicators and printers where the quality of the output was crucial. The quality of a copy or print is difficult to measure by the customer or on customer premises. The company in question, therefore, established what caused degradation of print quality and found that it depended crucially on the amount of light reaching the photoreceptor. This was something that can be effectively measured and this indirect measure enabled the company to ensure a high quality of output being maintained by taking preventive action when the amount of light began to fall off.

Flexibility Within a Standard Approach:

As we have said earlier, the standards should be developed from a company mission statement and cascade down through strategy and tactics to specific standards. By definition this makes the standard somewhat remote from the actual interface of the customer with the company, which is, after all, where the impact is made.

This apparently irreconcilable conflict can be resolved by leaving a great deal of freedom within the approach to provide a flexible support to customers to conform to their needs. Provided that everyone in the company understands what we are trying to achieve and the purpose of setting standards (in the setting of which most employees have hopefully been involved), we as managers should have sufficient confidence in our employees to allow some flexibility, with the understanding that any major deviation can subsequently be justified by the employee. This is where regular employee counselling is so important, which we will discuss in greater detail in the next chapter.

When we talk about "customer", it refers not only to the final user but to all internal customers as well. It is very difficult, if not impossible, to provide the final user with a product or service to an agreed standard, if all the intermediate internal customers have not done exactly the same. Total quality is dependent on each step being carried out to the agreed quality. Any necessary flexibility can be built in only at the last customer interface.

Internal and External Communication of Standards:

It is not good enough simply to establish reasonable standards for all company activities, these standards must be fully communicated to all staff. This is not as easy as it sounds, particularly in the management style currently employed by many companies. With narrowly defined goals often measured by the simplest method only (e.g. how many widgets, letters, invoices etc. have been produced in a given time), it is natural for quantity to replace satisfying customer needs as a priority.It is often difficult for one department in a company to understand the issues of another.

Although the need for clear communication is obvious, many companies do not plan to allow sufficient time to understand each other's problems and for staff to establish for themselves the problems involved in other parts of the company. Once these different parts of the company appreciate each other's issues, we will be in a position to satisfy internal customers and provide Total Quality to the end user. It will mean putting the whole company's interests before those of individual parts of it.

Top management will have to give a good example and be more open with its communication than it tends to be in many companies today. Frequently management at all levels keep information to themselves not because it is secret but because they believe that knowledge means power and not passing certain information on appears to give managers power. Free communication will make for a much smoother operation and leave management with sufficient time to do the job for which they are there, i.e. to lead and manage.

The other part of the communication process is to be proud of what we are doing and letting the customer know what we are providing. It is a fallacy to assume that the customer will notice himself that we are providing a superior support. He may, or he may not. It may be that one section of the customer's organisation is aware that we are providing a much better service than we used to but other areas, maybe even the decision makers, may not know of our success.

Communication with customers and blowing our own trumpet is necessary but we must be sure that we are really in a position to provide the Total Quality which we are promising to the customer. Some employees are reluctant to tell the customer the standards to which our company is working because they do not have the confidence in the whole organisation that the standards will be achieved and maintained.

This brings us back to the first part of the communication process, the internal communication. Internal communication is not only essential to understand each other's issues, we must also communicate achievements to build confidence within the whole company that the standards agreed are realistic, are being achieved and, if necessary reviewed and altered. This will build confidence in the organisation and employees will take pride to communicate the "good news" to the customer, in the knowledge that results will be achieved.

CHAPTER IX

The Human Aspect of Total Quality

Many companies have expended a great deal of their time and financial resources over the past decades modernising their production facilities and automating administrative and office procedures. These changes have been essential to stay in the competitive race.

An equally essential part of being competitive and being able to stay in business is to get all employees to contribute to the company's performance to the limit of their ability. Although conceptually this has been realised for a long time, only the most forward looking companies have, in the past, consistently worked at ensuring that the environment within their companies was conducive to a positive and enthusiastic climate within which employees' full contribution is achieved.

Senior management found it easier to deal with inanimate objects such as factory automation or office systems than with human beings. Performance of machines and systems is easier to define, to measure and to demonstrate a financial benefit than it is to deal with people, each one of whom has different needs, ambitions and desires. Despite the horror stories about breakdowns of machines and bugs in systems, the operation of this equipment is much more predictable than reactions of people. Management also find it easier to make decisions about objects where no personal sensitivities are involved than to interact with live human beings who have their own vested interests.

As the competitive battle is getting ever more fierce and the products or services offered are becoming more similar, it is the whole human aspect within a company which now needs to be addressed from a more holistic point of view. Companies can no longer move forward by merely firefighting in the area of industrial relations or accept anything but top performance. In fact, it will be almost impossible to ensure a Total Quality approach throughout a company over any length of time without concentrating more attention on the company's own employees.

Companies will not be able to "Service the Customer" if they do not first "Service their Employees". If we accept the inverted pyramid view of the market place (see Chapter V), where the workforce comes immediately below the customer, it is obvious that management has an essential task to act as facilitator to enable each employee to perform to the best of his or her ability.

So let us first look at some

Basic Human Behaviour Concepts

Behavioural scientists have spent their lifetimes studying and analysing these concepts and it is obviously not the purpose of this book to either review these studies or to try and develop new concepts. What will be useful in the context of Total Quality, however, will be to understand some of the most basic concepts on which most of the behavioural scientists agree although they may have expressed it in different ways.

What will make all of us do our work as effectively as possible is, what is generally called, "Motivation".

Each one of us is an individual and we are motivated by various factors in differing degrees. The level of motivation achieved will also change in each individual with time, circumstance, ambient conditions and other parameters.

The first thing we need to understand is what genuinely motivates people and what merely removes obstacles to motivation. The difference was most clearly explained by F. Herzberg when he suggested that we should look at various factors to see whether they were "Dis-satisfiers" (which he called "Hygiene Factors") or genuine "Satisfiers" (which he called "Motivating Factors). This is an important distinction to understand, because if we only concentrate on improving Hygiene Factors we may not achieve motivation.

Let me use an example. Let me assume that for my work in the company, say as an Accountant, I require an office, a desk and a chair. My employer informs me that there is a shortage of space and that it has been decided that I should use the corner of the warehouse as my office, use a large orange box as my desk and a small one as a chair. I would feel (as I was pulling splinters from my forearm and other parts of my body) that my work as an accountant was not appreciated, as I was asked to work in sub-standard conditions. I would be dissatisfied and my employer would find it difficult to motivate me.

This employer comes to his senses and transfers me to a very large, well lit and ventilated office, provides me with a large desk, a comfortable swivel chair, bookcases lining the walls, a coffee table with chairs and other desirable requisites. I would no longer be dissatisfied with my surroundings but, after the first week or two in my new office, I would not be specifically motivated by my office to perform to the best of my ability – it would just be "my office". It would no longer detract from my being receptive to genuine motivators, but it would not be a motivator in its own right.

So "Hygiene Factors" are necessary to enable an employee to be receptive to motivation, but once the appropriate level commensurate with the work being done is reached, further improvement will not positively motivate people. By analysing the various contributing factors it has been generally found that those factors directly concerned with work itself are often "Motivating Factors" whereas those concerned with the conditions of work are usually "Hygiene Factors".

Before examining motivation to achieve Total Quality in detail let us just look at one of the ambivalent factors – money. Is "Money" a hygiene factor or a motivating one. A great deal has been said and written on this subject, some of it contradictory. The most logical view is that "Money" falls into both areas: basic pay can be considered a "Hygiene Factor" as it is unlikely that a month or two after we received a substantial rise we will come to work and think to ourselves: "Last month I had a good rise, I will do a great job for my company today". However, incentives (commission, bonus, profit share, etc) can be classified as "Motivating Factors".

What is the difference between these two payments? A pound received from either source will buy the same amount of bread. The money received as an incentive is the result of achieving a specific goal or reaching an agreed target. It is task orientated. Usually these tasks are relatively short term tasks (up to a year). They are a recognition of an individual or a group achievement.

Just one last word about money. If basic pay is not a motivator, why do some companies pay more for equivalent jobs than others? Do they believe that a higher basic salary is motivating or is there some other reason? You will find that almost invariably the companies who pay above average salaries do so because they want to attract a wider range of applicants for initial interviews, to be able to choose better candidates and to retain them once they are on board and after the company has spent a great deal of resources in training these people.

So now we know that money as a motivator has a role to play but that that role is limited. What else can be used to motivate people? Almost all experts agree that it is the work content, the working climate, the opportunity to make full use of and develop one's skills and to be appreciated as a valuable member of the company team. As McClelland pointed out, all of us are motivated by a mixture of Achievement, Power and Affiliation. One other aspect which has come much more to the fore over the past decade is Dowling's findings that managers must "...promote the experience of understanding and invention, qualities shared by most human beings..." to motivate their staff.

So let us see how we can use these basic concepts in the practical world to

Motivate Staff to Achieve Total Qaulity

The first issue in most studies on the subject of motivation has revolved around "Achievement". Clearly, before I can get a feeling of achievement, I must know what it is that I am expected to achieve. This brings us immediately back into the area covered in the previous chapter on the subject of "Standards". Each employee has the right to get a clear indication from his superior of what is expected of him in his job.

In the context of Total Quality, therefore, the company's mission statement needs to be broken down into smaller and smaller units until the targets for the individual can be agreed between him and his superior. This will ensure not only that the individual knows what is expected of him but, and perhaps even more important, that this target will contribute to the achievement of the whole company's goals.

This will enable the individual to have a benchmark against which to measure his achievement and, at the same time, instil pride in his job as he will be able to see how his contribution assists the whole company to reach its goals. To work together with the team of his colleagues for the common good will also create a feeling of belonging and thus contribute towards a sense of affiliation.

For these achievements to be genuine motivators, the targets agreed should be challenging but attainable, they should be quantifiable wherever possible to ensure an objective measure and they should be regularly discussed with the superior during counselling sessions to see how progress towards achieving these goals is coming along.

While on the subject of regular counselling – this is a motivator in its own right. It does a number of other things to improve quality:

• The superior can demonstrate that there is no "Them and Us" in the company's approach in reaching its goals – his goals are achieved by each of his subordinates achieving their targets; the section's contribution is part of the department's goals etc. Therefore there is an identity of interests – the superior's counselling is genuinely intended to improve the quality of performance of the individual to reach the joint goal.

• It will help to improve the quality of the individual's performance.

• The regularity of counselling will ensure that the discussions are considered as constructive criticism by the employee and not resented as being destructive.

• It will demonstrate to the employee that his work is important in the context of the whole company's quality effort as his superior spends an adequate amount of time with him.

Excessive counselling could, however, be considered to be a lack of trust by the supervisor in the employee to be able to achieve his targets without such help. The skill of the manager, therefore, is to judge the correct level of counselling; not so little as to give the impression that the work of the individual is not important to the company and not too much to indicate a lack of confidence.

This is particularly important with the recent drive in many companies to reduce the number of management levels in their structure which often means increasing the span of control of managers which, in turn, may mean insufficient time for adequate and regular counselling. It is a question of prioritising the manager's tasks and if he accepts that the only way the Total Quality of his department's work will be achieved will be through his people, then he will create the time necessary to spend counselling them.

The ideal balance will also have to be found in other areas of support, be it through systems, technical support or spare parts. Taking each one of these separately, on systems the manager will have to balance the level of systems support with the danger of depersonalising the job. In the area of technical support this must be made readily available to staff and yet each individual must be given sufficient lattitude to develop his own skills. When it comes to spare parts, staff have the right to expect frequently used spares to be readily available but will appreciate that rarely used and expensive parts cannot be held at every stocking echelon.

All this balancing is a difficult task for management but it is an essential part of running an efficient operation and thus achieving Total Quality in every part of the operation.

Total Quality in itself is an important motivator for every employee. We all want to work for an efficient company which is creating customer satisfaction in the market. We also like to work for a successful company which can make us proud to work for it. So for this reason, too, management should openly communicate quality goals and progress towards achieving them with all their staff.

Customer satisfaction can be demonstrated to employees not only by publicising letters of commendation from customers – even though satisfied customers, alas, do not frequently write to their suppliers to praise the performance of the company or of employees – but by publicly recognising repeat orders, recommendations to other clients etc. as proof of customer satisfaction. You know yourselves how heart-warming it is to have satisfied a customer.

This brings me to my next essential point in motivating staff, i.e. recognition of achievement. It is satisfying to know that we have achieved our goals but it is important that this achievement is recognised by our superiors, by our peers and by the company as a whole. In many companies the achievements of some individuals and departments are highlighted regularly in company magazines or newsletters. Unfortunately, it is easier to highlight good performance by, say, a salesman than to do so for an order clerk or warehouseman. Yet all of them contribute to the customer's perception of Total Quality.

One of the main reasons why salemen's results are highlighted more often in company magazines and newsletters than that of other employees is the fact that their results are more visible and readily available to the editor of the journal. It is the task of the manager to make it easy for the editor to obtain data on quality performance of employees in departments where the information is not quite as accessible as sales results.

That means that the manager must keep the editor informed or, better still, draft the article for him.

While we are talking about the job satisfaction of our employees in motivating them towards achieving Total Quality we should also look at the whole area of work contents. Particularly in areas where repetitive jobs are involved, ways have to be found to make the job more interesting to ensure high quality of performance throughout the day. One of the most effective ways of achieving this is through job enrichment. There are many ways of restructuring jobs to attain this. One of the most widely used ones is job rotation which has the added benefit of giving our staff a better insight into the operation of the department or company and makes the operation more flexible. Another effective way of job enrichment is by enlarging the job contents by making the employee cover a wider range of tasks or, alternatively, by giving him increasing knowledge or skills in a narrow task (generalist versus specialist).

Each one of us gets his job satisfaction in different ways and it is the manager's skill in identifying individuals' needs and matching these with company requirements. It is not an easy job but I am sure that noone ever told you that motivating staff or, for that matter, management is an easy job.

In some company activities the work load fluctuates steeply; at peak time staff is overloaded whereas in trough periods there is insufficient work for our staff. Both an overload as well as insufficient work makes it difficult to motivate our staff towards high quality performance. The skill of the manager again consist in identifying the causal factors for this fluctuation which may well give him advance warning when it is likely to occur. Once he has got this basic information he can take management action to smooth the workload. All of us will feel stressed if the overload is excessive and if we only have four hours work to do in a $7^1/_2$ hour day, we will feel demotivated.

Job enrichment can often assist managers to balance workloads in various departments, particularly if not all of the tasks are highly time sensitive. It just requires basic data, some creative thinking, knowledge of your staff and obtaining their cooperation.

This brings us into the area mentioned by Wm. Dowling quoted earlier in this chapter, i.e. promoting the experience of understanding and invention. How can we, as managers, use the full capabilities of our employees if, perhaps, their jobs are narrow and humdrum? First we must realise that each of our employees is a thinking individual who genuinely wants to contribute to the best of his ability to further the aims of the company. In general, we tend to underestimate the intellectual capabilities of our staff and their desire to perform to the highest quality.

Secondly, we should accept that the employee himself who is doing the job day in and day out probably has considered other ways of doing his work, or for that matter other tasks in the company, more efficiently. No-one has, however, given him the opportunity of expressing his idea or voicing his opinion. True, he may not be aware how any proposed change may affect other parts of the company but if his proposal is beneficial, it may be worthwhile to make changes elsewhere in the company as well. We need to listen carefully to what our employees have to say.

This may not only improve motivation of the employee (because there are few higher compliments than that someone is interested in what we have to say) but we as managers are in danger of really learning something! If we then adopt the proposal and give the individual public credit for having come up with a good idea, you will find that this will motivate not only the individual concerned but also other employees to come up with suggestions.

These suggestions can be generated by informal means as mentioned above (in discussion), or by more formal methods such as suggestion schemes and Quality Circles (see Chapter II). A study was recently done by one of the professional association into the effectiveness of suggestion schemes among its member firms. A correlation study was then performed to establish what succesful schemes had in common. Surprisingly, it was not the amount of the reward that was offered for successful suggestions which was highly important but the efficiency with which the scheme is administered. Well administered schemes, where a tight feedback loop to originators of suggestions was established, were highly successful.

Often a manager is not aware of the capabilities of his subordinates; he sees them perform only in their assigned tasks and he finds it difficult to imagine them in other areas. Even experienced individuals trained to recognise certain qualities sometimes find it difficult to imagine a person performing in a different role. This message was brought home to me very early in my life while I was still at school. My House had elected me to captain the football team and some time later when I captained the school team the headmaster said to me: "I realised that you were a reasonable footballer but I thought your House had made a mistake in electing you captain as you never showed any leadership qualities on the field until you were in the position to demonstrate it". That is the problem for most managers, to envisage their employees perform in other roles.

Let us now turn to opportunities for promotion. You will note that I have carefully stated "Opportunities" for promotion rather than "Promotion". What is highly demotivating to all members of a department or of a company is for all management positions being always filled from outside the department or outside the company. It demonstrates a lack of confidence of management in their employees and, of course, also reflects adversely on their own choice of staff, if for all promotions they have to resort to outside sources. Clearly there is a benefit in having some influx of new ideas by recruiting management from outside to cross-fertilise the existing skills but it is not conducive to motivation to have no internal promotional opportunities.

All of us need to have self-esteem to be motivated into achieving a high quality of output. One of the most effective ways of increasing self-esteem is for managers to involve their staff in decisions affecting their work – in a way I am reiterating the need for listening to our employees. But involvement is more than that, it is making them feel an integral part of the decision making process. It is taking nothing away from the manager; he will take the final decision but by involving his staff in the discussion he will ensure first of all that he will have a wide choice of options to consider, secondly that his staff will be motivated and thirdly that implementation of the decision will be much more thorough and carried out with greater enthusiasm than if he merely issues an instruction.

The complexity of a modern business no longer allows a manager to take his decisions in isolation. He is not able to be close enough to every part of the operation to judge the effect of every decision on it and to establish any remedial activities which may be necessary to obtain Total Quality benefits rather than merely narrow functional ones.

This brings us back to the fact that

Total Quality is a Powerful Motivator

Not only do all of us feel more comfortable working for a company whose products or services and their total image in the market-place is that of a high quality company, but if we have a feeling of pride in our company and its products, services and staff we will also be motivated to do everything possible to reinforce this image. We will be helping our colleagues to ensure that their part of the total task is done effectively as we know that only by each individual's output is performed to the agreed quality will we be able to maintain our quality image.

Once this pride in Total Quality has been engendered throughout the company, it is likely that every member of the company will guard the reputation most jealously and take initiatives himself if necessary. There are any number of stories of "Corporate Heroism" where individuals at every level in the company hierarchy have performed tasks beyond the call of duty just to maintain the company's reputation for Total Quality.

This is the type of spirit managers need to develop in their staff to ensure that nothing but the best is acceptable which, in turn, will motivate everyone else to put everything into assuring Total Quality.

This will not happen by itself – it will need a great deal of thinking, planning and implementing before Total Quality will be achieved. This is a never ending task, as improvements are always possible. In fact, part of motivation comes not only from achieving improvements but from a desire to strive to reach ever higher goals.

CHAPTER X

Planning and Implementing Total Quality

We have already established that Total Quality is everybody's business within a company and not only that of a selected few who have been specifically designated to coordinate activities in that field. In view of the fact that everyone in the company and every department and function is involved with it, the direction for achieving it must be driven from the top.

Top Management's Role

To ensure an integrated company-wide approach to Total Quality, the impetus must start from the top. The Chief Executive must be convinced that the success of his organisation depends on the complete satisfaction of customers with all the products, services and support that is provided by the company and that this can only be achieved by all tasks being performed to the specified quality.

As Mr. John F. Akers, Chairman of I.B.M. put it so eloquently at the 1989 Annual General Meeting in Pittsburgh, Pennsylvania:

> "IBM must become a company in which the customer is, in every single decision, the final arbiter – the company that exercises selectivity in the markets it pursues and dedicates itself to market leadership...that is responsive to customer needs...that will not rest until every single customer is not just satisfied, but delighted with every association with IBM.

If we can do all these things, and I believe we can, then everything else important – market share, revenue, profit returns, and stockholder value – will follow"

This is the type of message that needs to be communicated throughout the company. That is, however, only the first step. A mere statement from the top may set the direction in which a company will satisfy its customers through Total Quality but actions are required:

– the whole process needs to be planned, and a strategy must be developed (BS 5750 mentioned in Chapter II is one of the effective disciplines which can be used)

– people need to be involved, trained, educated and convinced that management means to see its words transformed into concerted activities in every division, department and section of the company

– the enthusiasm created by the earlier actions need to be continuously sustained

– the necessary targets need to be agreed to ensure interfunctional goals do not conflict with one another

– the results must be monitored not only by internal, company measures but by customer perceived improvements

– the work of satisfying customers is never completed; customer expectations change and so we must always strive to improve our customer support

You will see from this short summary of some of the major tasks which need to be undertaken that this will require effort and resources throughout the company. The only group of people who can authorise and drive this type of major undertaking is top management itself.

This does not mean that top management needs to be involved in every step of the process. It does mean, however, that it must be fully involved, and seen to be involved, with the programme.

Top management can delegate most tasks to designated executives but they cannot abrogate their responsibility for ensuring that Total Quality becomes a way of life throughout the company. Customer Satisfaction should be included in the job specification of departmental managers and section heads and top management must measure the performance of these managers by their contribution to Customer Satisfaction.

In some companies, senior managers have to earn part of their bonus by achieving clearly stated customer satisfaction targets and it is said to be the intention of top management to gradually extend this system down the management ladder to the whole company.

This type of action by top management will make people throughout the company strive to improve their support to their internal or external customers both for selfish reasons (opportunity for increasing their bonus), but also because it demonstrates that top management really means business when they talk about satisfying customers through quality performance by every member of staff. It is converting mere platitudes into company goals.

In consequence, the role of top management is primarily to set direction, make the necessary initial resources available, appoint suitable staff to coordinate activities throughout the company and review progress at regular intervals.

Let me make it quite clear again, the fact that top management is establishing a department to coordinate quality programmes throughout the company does not mean that functional heads do not remain responsible for the quality performance of their function and staff. The line managers carry the responsibility for the quality performance of their activities. The new department, let us call it Customer Service Department for convenience of communication, is there as a resource to assist functional managers to monitor customer satisfaction levels, and to coordinate activities within the company to ensure that the desired level of customer support and quality of product or service is attained.

A Total Quality strategy is an integral part of the whole strategic approach of the company and cannot be developed in isolation. Top management will need a great deal of background information of where the company's products or services stand in the perception of customers and how important the various paramaters are to the customer. It will need to have an idea of how it compares with the competition for each of these parameters and from that a decision can be made which competitor should be utilised as a bench-mark for specific parameters.

Only then can an effort be made to decide where the company should aim to be; this will depend on its culture, its position in the market, its stage of development, and its mission. From this a strategy can be developed to reach the specified goal in a number of clearly defined steps, the attainment of each of these steps being carefully monitored.

It is usually advisable to look at the Total Quality activity in two separate but interlinked steps:

1. The quality of the product or service provided by the company. Basically, this looks at the way the process works.

2. The quality or suitability of the process itself. This step is designed to improve the way the process is constructed. This often leads to streamlining the interfaces between "internal" customers.

As this is likely to lead to a fundamental review of the activities of each function, the visible support of top management and full cooperation and recognition of ownership of senior management is essential.

Top management should demand regular status reports together with recommendations for action from the manager of the Customer Service Department. Top management does not need more problems, it probably has enough of those as it is, what it needs is a recommendation of how the resolution of the issue should be approached. This brings me to the next section:

Developing a Coherent Quality Programme

At first sight, the task for the Customer Service Manager will appear to be insurmountable. In consequence, he will have to approach the issue in a logical, carefully planned manner. He will have to convince each member of the company that change is a natural process – it is

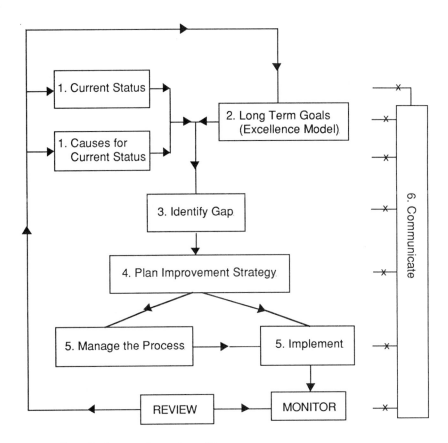

Figure 5: Developing a coherent quality programme

not a criticism of the way the work has been undertaken until now; it may well have been the best way to do the work at the time the process was introduced but with changing conditions inside and outside the company each member of the company should get a feeling of dissatisfaction with today's quality of products and services and with the process itself. Things can always be made better.

Before we look at details of developing and implementing a programme, let us first examine the process (see fig.5). The first step must obviously be to look at where the company stands now:

1. Analysis

Most companies have a great deal of information available about their markets, their customers, their competitors and their own strengths and weaknesses. The trouble is that this information is often scattered throughout the company and used only by a limited number of functions and not utilised in a coordinated, customer oriented manner.

This information is usually collected to support existing individual company processes rather than examining in depth what the *customer* really required. It needs to concentrate on outside influences rather than be excessively inward looking. The input should be as unbiased as possible and it needs to establish customers' opinions in a wide range of company's support activities – not only the quality of the company's products or services (the prime offering) is important but also their opinion of the quality of support activities. For example, the prime offering of an airline is to move people safely from one place to another at an acceptable price. The support activities involve items such as ease of buying tickets, ease of check-in, friendly and caring staff, clean aircraft, reasonable snacks and meals, etc.

This analysis stage should also examine the quality of support of internal customers which will automatically lead to looking at the effectiveness of the process itself. The final customer and user is unlikely to be able to get the best possible support if the intermediate stages are not performed to the highest quality, i.e. the internal customer is given the appropriate support all the time; this means providing 100% of the agreed quality every time.

2. Set Target

The company has now established where it stands in the eyes of its customers, be they internal or external. It knows how well it is doing in comparison with its competitors and in comparison to customer expectations.

From the analysis of the current situation, the company needs to agree where it wants to be at a specific time in the future. If the date is too far ahead, the "outside world" is likely to have changed and the company will therefore have to forecast the context in which it will be operating at that time. For instance, we all know that the European

Commission is developing a number of directives which will affect the customer support in a few years' time and the company needs to set its targets with that in mind.

It will also help if the long term aims can be broken down into a number of discreet steps, each of which has its own targets and measures; these must be monitored for achieving the desired results. It is then possible to re-evaluate the longer-term goals with the experience of the current activities in mind.

Once the opportunities for improvement have been identified it will be necessary to identify the resources (financial, human, time) required to progress activities. Total quality may require some front end investments, but in the medium and longer term it will show substantial benefits.

3. Identify the Gap

In stage 1 the current position was analysed, in stage 2 the desired long-term and intermediate goals have been set. Step 3 then moves to identifying the gap between these two positions. The gap needs to be broken down in such a way that a plan can be made for a group of functions, individual functions or sub-functions to progress towards the desired goals.

4. Planning the Activities

Having identified the changes that need to take place (step 3), specific tasks must be allocated to working groups to come up with plans of how the targets are to be reached. As we will see in the next sub-section on "Involvement", the solution to issues are best reached by a joint activity of the staff involved rather than by dictate from above. This planning process will not only propose plans for resolving problems but it will also assess any potential obstacles likely to be encountered.

For each activity it will be necessary to

a. Identify the customer
b. Identify the output
c. Identify and agree customer needs
d. Translate these needs into a "product" specification

e. Identify the steps in the work process

f. Select and agree measurement criteria

g. Determine capabilities and resource requirements

5. Managing the Process and Implementation

Once some of the activities have been carefully planned as set out in step 4 above, care must be taken that the activities agreed within a specific group are fully communicated to other parts of the company. Changes proposed by one group may adversely affect the work of another, who may not have been directly involved in the preparation of these plans.

The work of these groups must, therefore be coordinated across all affected areas and management must take the final decision as to whether to proceed with the proposed changes. Management then makes the necessary resources available for individual steps and agrees to the monitoring procedure - these measures must be agreed prior to the start of the implementation stage.

Only then can implementation of any of the plans commence. This is a crucial stage of the process because it is possible that certain unexpected obstacles arise and need to be removed or alleviated prior to proceeding with the project as initially planned. In many companies management who have helped in developing improvement plans lose interest at the implementation stage, and get involved with the more exciting planning stage for the next project.

Yet it is the efficient implementation of these plans which will result in the improvements, not the plans in themselves. It is essential that implementation is carefully managed, that activities adhere to the plans and that only approved changes to the plans are incorporated.

From bitter experience I can tell you that many an excellent customer support plan has fallen by the wayside not because it was a bad plan or that the results were not achievable, but simply because during its implementation unauthorised changes were introduced which invalidated the whole project. In a major study the writer has undertaken comparing service of Japanese companies with those of Western companies, the major difference was not that the Japanese companies had more or better programmes, but rather that the programmes they did have were more thoroughly implemented. Probably the best example of this is the Statistical Process Control approach to quality discussed in Chapter II.

During the implementation stage, each activity needs to be carefully monitored; this means not only measuring against the internally set targets but, wherever possible, evaluating the results in customer perception. This will lead to a review of the process and to a review of the activities involved.

6. Communication

An essential part of the whole process is to keep everyone informed of the progress of the whole programme. This does not mean flooding people with detailed data – it is as easy to keep people uninformed by giving them too much information as it is by not giving them any. What is necessary, however, is to provide each level of management with the appropriate level of data and keep each working group informed of what is going on in other areas of the company and to feed back to each group progress on their own projects.

A regular review process should be set up with top management to ensure its continued involvement with the programme, to compare actuals against plans and to identify any benefits achieved. Wherever a major project is being reviewed, it is highly recommended to involve a member of the project team in the presentation, or at least to assure his presence during the discussion. This will be both motivational to the staff concerned and will demonstrate better than anything else the continued interest of top management in improving Total Quality.

Involving Staff

All members of the company must feel that Total Quality is something to which they, personally, contribute. A voluntary involvement in analysing and progressing relevant issues is therefore a natural way of generating this feeling.

Furthermore, these members of the staff have been doing the relevant work for various periods of time and it would be surprising, if they did not have valuable solutions to contribute in resolving identified issues or raising points which have not even been thought of until that time.

In this connection it is essential that each member of staff feels free to contribute his ideas without fear of being penalised for putting it forward. In many cases highly beneficial improvements have been squashed by short-sighted managers who felt that any major change reflected adversely on the way their department was currently operating. They must understand that lack of change, being (or pretending to be) satisfied with the present processes and operating under yester-year's conditions, will in the long run jeopardise the competitiveness of their company and the security of their own job.

This does not mean that managers will not continue to manage - they will manage in a somewhat different way. They will manage the company in a customer oriented manner, to achieve the optimum level of customer satisfaction with an attractive profit for the company – this can only be achieved by Total Quality throughout every part of the organisation.

This will also entail listening to their staff for proposals of how the various activities could be undertaken more efficiently, changed drastically or even eliminated. This listening process includes not only the hearing of the words spoken by their staff but making a genuine effort to understand the intent of the communication and genuinely evaluating its applicability to the task in hand.

It will mean that managers will no longer try and defend past procedures but that they will look ahead at how these activities can be improved. Senior and top management will have to think of change as a way of life and to reward managers for positive efforts to improve results. Until now suggestions from first line managers to streamline their operations and reduce activities have too often been rewarded by the downgrading of the department and the manager concerned. Managers have to be discouraged from building empires and those who can achieve the same results with lower resources must be commended.

The involvement of staff will be the most difficult task to introduce in the whole Total Quality approach. Most companies' culture is currently oriented towards the concept that the "thinking" is done by the managers and the "doing" by staff. Managers will have to learn to understand that their staff have extensive combined skills, knowledge and experience and that neglecting to tap this source will limit the effectiveness of any programme.

It may also mean that resources will need to be re-allocated between departments. Let me give you a few examples. In a number of companies the whole distribution, inventory control and transportation system was reviewed and it was found that substantial savings to the whole company could be achieved by reducing the number of warehouses, resulting in a reduction of running costs and inventory, but incurring increased transportation costs. At the same time the level of service to customers was substantially improved, providing added value to the customer and reducing company costs. This did mean a major re-allocation of resources. Modern and more efficient management tools had to be introduced to be more responsive to customer orders, staff had to be suitably trained, a major logistic reduction of warehouses had to be planned and transportation costs, both internal and from outside contractors, were substantially increased. Both the direct benefits (reduced total costs and improved level of service) and the indirect benefits (increased turnover and morale) were substantial.

In other companies the Total Quality approach has meant a complete change of how customer contact is handled. With the introduction of a Customer Information Centre (see also Chapter XI, Management Tools) companies have been able to improve the support to customers over the telephone while reducing their costs of unnecessary visits by sales and service staff. By using a telemarketing approach they were able to resolve customer issues immediately or at least to qualify enquiries from customers, making the contact between salesmen and customers more productive. On the service side many apparent product problems are merely due to faulty operation by the customer which can often be resolved over the telephone and even certain product problems can be overcome in this way.

In both these examples it meant that resources between departments had to be reviewed and it was possible to do so only by the detailed involvement of staff from a number of different functions.

The drive for Total Quality must emphasise that a company's future success depends not on the efficiency of a specific department, but on the most effective way to satisfy customers and this involves the whole company. The whole-hearted contribution from everyone is therefore essential.

Creating Enthusiasm

As we have just seen we need the whole-hearted support from everyone in the company to achieve a coordinated approach to Total Quality throughout the whole organisation. We therefore need to create enthusiasm for the programme and, moreover, sustain this enthusiasm over long periods of time.

The considerations on motivation which we examined in the previous chapter should be of help to us in this context.

First and foremost, all of us like to be appreciated for the contributions that we are making to the company's success. In consequence, involvement, which we have just discussed, will also help us to create enthusiasm.

All of us like to work for a successful company and contribute to successful programmmes. Many companies do not keep their staff adequately informed in this respect. Only selected members of staff are kept informed of company achievements. Senior management in these companies often maintain that their staff would not understand business or financial data which would illustrate success of the company. This may be so, but if staff is educated in these matters by their immediate superiors, they will not only understand the information but feel much more part of the company and contribute enthusiastically in pushing it to the forefront and keeping it there.

Success breeds success. This is not just a saying but a fact of life. We have already mentioned that progress of individual quality projects should be publicised and this will also create enthusiasm. A photograph of the Managing Director shaking the hand (or presenting a prize) to a member of staff who has put forward a worthwhile suggestion will do wonders in creating enthusiasm in staff for a Quality programme. We all like to work for a company who provides the customer with quality products and services.

Another effective way of creating enthusiasm for a Total Quality programme is to arrange for management and staff from departments who do not normally visit customers to call on them on a pre-arranged basis and discuss with the user the company's products and services in general and the effect of their contribution specifically. On return to their work-place they should be encouraged to give a short talk to their colleagues, who may not have had the opportunity of such a visit as yet, at the next departmental meeting.

In some companies enthusiasm is generated by offering rewards for proposals which are subsequently implemented. If this approach is taken, the fairness of the reward system must be clearly demonstrable and should be published before putting the scheme into effect.

Most important part of all, senior and top management have to demonstrate that the Total Quality programme is not a "Here today and gone tomorrow" activity but that it is here to stay. It is a project which they, as senior and top management, fully support, not only by words but in their day to day decision making process. The approach must be consistent and seen to be so.

Visibility needs to be maintained throughout to ensure that other priorities do not displace Total Quality as the essential goal to retain customer loyalty and gain additional clients.

Communicating Progress

We touched on this subject in step 6 of the planning process and the remarks are equally applicable at the later stage of implementation.

Now we have targets which have been agreed by the parties concerned. It is easy for "internal" customers to get together and agree standards and targets to which they will work. It is getting more and more usual for a similar "agreement" to be reached with outside customers, particularly where the vendor supplies the same customer regularly. It is very usual under these condition for the two parties to sit down together and agree very detailed quality targets not only of the prime product and service but also for support activities.

Where this is not the case, these quality targets are developed from customer requirements and converted into meaningful internal company targets.

Companies who have established this type of target obviously monitor their achievement and the result on customer perceived quality. This information, however, is often not fed back to the people who have contributed to achieving these results. They are only made available on a "need to know" basis.

It will be difficult to sustain enthusiasm for a Total Quality programme or to ensure a continuous striving for improvements, if results are not communicated effectively throughout the company. Some companies are very active in propagating results but there are still many who restrict the distribution of this information.

Besides the formal methods of feedback, companies utilise their House Magazines or Newsletters to keep staff informed of progress and in some large groups of companies a special Bulletin Sheet is published at regular intervals tracking results in general and highlighting specific achievement of divisions or departments in detail, describing the initial situation and the new improvements and how they were attained. They also point out pitfalls which had to be overcome on the way to assist other functions or divisions in avoiding the same mistakes.

CHAPTER XI

Management Tools to Increase Customer Satisfaction

In the past, technology has primarily been used to make the production or administrative processes more efficient and, in this way, some indirect benefits to the customer were achieved. Examples of this are the mechanisation of the production of many products which has indirectly contributed to customer satisfaction by keeping costs and prices under control and improving the consistency of the product quality to the customer. In the office similar indirect benefits were achieved by automating the work and by speeding up customer support.

In most of these cases the impetus for management to introduce these modern methods have been internal, i.e. the streamlining of manufacturing or administrative processes.

A more recent driver for introducing modern management tools into companies has been the direct benefit to customers through improving the quality of the support activities.

It is important to understand these two reasons for introducing modern technologies into a company although the division between the two is being increasingly blurred, i.e. the improvements introduced to improve customer satisfaction are also helping the company to serve itself better, and vice versa.

Some Management Tools for Customer Support

The major technologies which have helped to improve the tools used by companies to support their customers are largely based on computers and telecommunication. These two technologies are being increasingly interlinked and combined in complete customer support systems.

This does not mean that other technologies are not being developed for assisting companies to improve the quality of their customer support. These include electronics in its broadest sense, optical and laser developments as well as more efficient utilisation of chemical films, electronic video and audio tapes and the more creative application of electro-mechanical and automotive technology.

The choice of management tool to be used to improve customer satisfaction will largely depend on the analysis of customer requirements and the affordability of introducing the modern tool. The immense progress that has been made in this area over the past few years has been brought about by the substantial reduction of cost of introducing these tools. Not only has the cost of computer hardware come down in leaps and bounds but whereas in the past companies may have had to develop their own software programs to support the desired activities, a great number of these programs are now being made available off the shelf. The documentation is usually sufficiently good for companies to make necessary adjustments in-house to fit individual needs.

The important part of the exercise is to keep customer orientation foremost in the decision of how to streamline the operation. In too many instances the initial intent is to satisfy customer needs but once the detailed work of deciding what tools to use has been done, the original purpose of the exercise is forgotten and only internal company needs are satisfied. If the customer is to be directly involved in using the tool (e.g. a bank's money dispenser), it must be highly user friendly and reliable.

The human aspect of using automation must also not be forgotten. Customers often want the opportunity to discuss their issues with a live person – at other times they prefer the convenience of getting their needs fulfilled as quickly as possible, at all times of the day or night. In the latter case, a piece of equipment, be it a drinks dispenser or a cash point, is preferred.

The effect on companies' own staff must also not be forgotten. In addition to the inherent resistance to change, staff genuinely must have some contact with their colleagues. In a number of instances, companies have gone too far in automating their processes and members of their staff never had an opportunity of talking to their colleagues. This led to a drop in morale which counteracted the benefit the companies promised themselves from the introduction of technology. A happy balance is required and, before introducing the new management tools, the project should be fully discussed with the staff who are to use them.

The cost reduction management tools are so well entrenched by now that we need not spend time on reviewing them (e.g. for invoicing, administration, record keeping, filing, word processing, planning, etc.).

The customer orientated tools which have been introduced over the past few years and which have given companies cost benefits at the same time are probably of more interest. Many of them are based on the realisation that customers are not interested in specific technologies but in the resolution of their issues. The more competitive industries had to examine the quality of their customer support more urgently; some have resolved the issues more efficiently than others. It most cases the real customer benefits come from a combination of activities.

Let us now look at some specific industries. One with which all of us get involved at some time or other is food shopping. The growth of supermarkets has changed our shopping habits. They have chosen locations convenient for customers, provided adequate parking facilities (in most instances) and have provided their staff with management tools with which they can efficiently support customers. At the "sharp end", the check-out has been streamlined by introducing barcode pricing which can be quickly read and transformed into a customer bill.

The customer, however, also wants to be assured that the goods he wishes to buy in the supermarket are available when he wants them and the above billing system, i.e. the only "tool" visible to the customer, is linked to a sophisticated inventory control and replenishment system to ensure the customer will find what he needs. If he has to do part of his shopping elsewhere, some of the convenience of a single point shopping is lost and the company is also likely to lose not only the profit on the sale of that item but the customer is likely to buy other items in the second outlet as well.

As we have just touched on the subject of inventory control and distribution, management tools for this area have improved the planning abilities of companies and the results reported by some of them by the efficient use of these tools have given them a marketing advantage over their competitors. They have been able to increase the logistic level of service (LOLOS) to their customers by ensuring that a higher percentage of goods are available to them on first demand. At the same time many of them have been able to reduce the number of supply centres.

Other companies use sophisticated support tools to enable them to satisfy a variable customer demand for ambulances, taxis, service engineers, spare parts, telephone lines, etc. From past experience they can determine a pattern of activity that is likely to be required at any particular time under varying operating conditions. These management tools enable them to take management action to smoothe the peaks and troughs of customer demands. Many of these systems enable the company to realise that they may have difficulties in meeting their predetermined standards before they are in the actual situation and some action is still possible to avoid reducing the quality of their support. If a company is serious about Total Quality they must consider this type of approach.

Other tools have been developed to facilitate territory planning and to be able to analyse the effect of any changes on their customer support. In some companies it has been found that a large part of extended delivery times to customers were caused not by long manufacturing lead times, but by the excessive time necessary to process orders, clarify issues with customers, check credit ratings and fit in with artificially imposed internal company barriers. By utilising modern management tools they have been able to reduce delivery cycles by substantial periods without changing manufacturing processes.

Banks, insurance companies and building societies have also commenced utilising management tools to a greater extent to support customers. Most customers can get information on their balances just by enquiring, issues can be processed much more rapidly and further major changes are being field tested.

More and more staff are no longer required to make the long journey to their work-place every day of the week. With modern management tools "networking" is increasing, enabling staff to access the company's data base through a modem connected to their home (or portable) work-station. This reduces the pressure on valuable office space in the office, cuts travel time for the employee and improves the whole environment by reducing the number of commuters. Here again, a balance needs to be found between operational efficiency and the human desire for personal contact.

Service to customers can be improved by salesmen or office staff providing the customer with up-to-date information on pricing, the stock position, progress on orders, product features and capabilities from a central information centre which can substantially increase the effective time of salesmen in the field.

Creative Use of Management Tools to Gain a Marketing Advantage

Forward looking management in many companies have decided to utilise their management tools not only for gaining indirect customer benefits through streamlining their operations but to utilise these tools as a specific marketing tool.

Probably one of the earliest, extensive use of this approach was the well-known approach by American Airlines to seat reservation by travel agents throughout the U.S.A. mentioned in Chapter III.

Another example of the use of modern technology as a positive marketing tool is the General Electric Answer Centre in Louisville, Ky., which is said to be the largest consumer information centre in the world. It is available to customers, as well as to GE's own staff, for 24 hours, 365 days a year. They handle about 120 product lines and 8500 different models. Obviously the workload varies between days of the week and hours of the day – it varies from about 15 calls per hour to more than 1500 calls per hour. The individual operators' terminals are linked to remote mainframe computers. The data is continually analysed for change in patterns of work and type of enquiry and the various operating units analyse the information for guidance to changes in products or support activities. Customers have reacted very favourably to this facility. Some of GE's competitors had to follow their example – what greater flattery can be bestowed on a project?

The American Hospital Supply Corporation, a large distributor of hospital requirements, has enabled customers to have a direct link into the order entry, order progressing and dispatching system. This has enabled them to give better service to their customers while reducing their level of inventory. Customers found it so much more convenient to do business through this system that turnover increased substantially.

Hewlett-Packard opened their Customer Information Centre (CIC) in Atlanta, Georgia in 1988 to replace a number of local centres. The CIC enabled both customers and employees to obtain immediate up to date information on pricing, order status, configuration control, and access to all technical and commercial information. It also helped the sales force by validating and qualifying leads; salesmen were equipped with portable computers which increased their selling time by 27%, reduced travel by 13% and increased order performance by 10%. It increased salesmen's confidence and professional image and, therefore, also their motivation. The most important benefit was the increased customer satisfaction by having their queries answered immediately.

It is not only American businesses which creatively use modern management tools. Akzo Coatings of Holland have improved their car parts and repair business substantially by being able to access spares listings of about 2000 models from various makers, as well as repair procedures and a guideline to labour hours required for the repair. This enables their outlets to quote customers an accurate price for the repair cost which obviously gave them a marketing advantage.

Marks & Spencer in the U.K. have been able to free many square metres of valuable sales space in the centres of large cities by developing a distribution and inventory control system, enabling them to replenish items bought from these stores at short notice and thus freeing the space previously used for storing goods for the purpose this space was intended for, i.e. to sell goods to customers.

You need not be a very large organisation to be creative in using management tools developed for streamlining your activities to get a marketing advantage by using these tools pro-actively. The Computer Cab Company of London, who controls the movement of about one third of London's taxis, developed a very efficient and sophisticated movement control system. The customer telephones an operator who logs details of the incoming call which is passed automatically to the dispatcher who controls the movement of the taxis. In addition to small and casual users, the company also serves a number of large users who make continuous use of taxis. By providing some of these customers with a terminal which enabled them to by-pass the initial operator who logs details of the call, they not only saved the time of the operator to log and enter the details, but gave the customer a number of advantages: he did not have to wait till an operator was available and could enter the system direct. This speeded up the ordering of the taxi, thus by-passing one step and resulting in a faster response. This company also demonstrated its customer orientation by enabling account customers to get their invoices broken down by customer specified cost centres, saving large customers a great deal of time when the invoice was received.

The thought I would like to leave you with in this section is that the range of customer services your company can supply is only limited by the creativity of your thinking and the genuine wish to provide customers with Total Quality in every contact with the customer – in fact an attitude of mind which continually searches for more effective ways of satisfying customers. In the medium and longer term this will improve company profits.

CHAPTER XII

Spreading Total Quality to Suppliers

Once our company has accepted the Total Quality concept it will become obvious that the full benefit can only be achieved if the same determination to perform every task to the quality required by the customer is also introduced to the suppliers who are providing products and services to our company.

In some contexts, this will be self-evident. For instance, when Sir John Egan took over the running of Jaguar Cars and decided to put the improvement of quality of the product at the top of Jaguar's priorities, a detailed study of customer complaints showed that over half of the complaints from users could be traced back to components bought from sub-contractors. It is obviously very expensive to build faulty components into a car and then to have to replace them under warranty – it does not help to improve the reputation of the car manufacturer either! It is also not very beneficial for component manufacturers to deliver, say, 100 components and have 30 of them sent back by the car manufacturer when they are found to be faulty during inspection on arrival at the assembly plant.

It is clearly the responsibility of the initial component manufacturer to construct his production process in such a way that the quality of all components remains within the set standard. In this context many buyers insist on the vendors to receive a BS5750 certification which will give the purchaser confidence that the process conforms to recognised standards. If a vendor cannot maintain the agreed standards, he is unlikely to remain a supplier to the company using these components in its assembly process. The incentive for the vendor to produce products and services to agreed standards is the privilege of remaining a supplier.

A study carried out by Marks & Spencer (M&S) some years ago showed that 10% of the cost of products was spent on inspection. They decided to eliminate incoming inspection completely. Detailed discussions with the manufacturers before products are purchased ensure that effort spent in the pre-production run make it unnecessary for M&S to inspect products; the responsibility rests entirely with the manufacturer. M&S only test products in use by user panels consisting of their own staff and that of the manufacturers. Manufacturers' staff tend to be the most critical customers of their own products. Complaints are used very actively to improve future supplies.

It is not only the quality of the product which is so important to a long-term relationship between sub-contractors and the company. With the world-wide drive for minimising inventories of both semi-manufactured and finished articles, the OEM (original equipment manufacturer, or user of the components) must be able to rely not only on the quality of the parts, products or services he is buying, but also the anciliary offering of the supplier, such as delivery, technical support, packaging, etc. It is therefore the quality of every activity of the supplier, or total quality, that is needed.

The benefits of this approach for the buyer can easily be appreciated but what are the

Benefits to the Supplier

Initial thoughts of many suppliers were that the only benefit which they were likely to achieve by this pressure from their customers for a consistently high quality was the opportunity to remain a supplier to the company but that this approach would cut into their profit margins. In practice it was found that by doing the job right first time, cut wastage very considerably and it has enabled suppliers to maintain and in most cases to increase profit margins and improve the level of service to their customers.

Few companies have made detailed studies of what the lack of quality is costing but it is estimated by experts in this area that the average cost of lack of quality across business and industry is as high as 30%, much higher in some companies and lower in others. This loss of efficiency commences inside the supplier's company. A lack of confidence in the support provided by other departments or functions means that their output is checked and counterchecked by user departments, some of the work is returned to the previous work station for rework. Worst of all, mistakes are not spotted and further work is carried out on the assumption that the faulty output from the previous activity is right, and additional resources are wasted before the mistake is discovered. If the product or service is then supplied to a customer, a great deal more resources are wasted in returning the goods, in allocating responsibilities, extensive administrative expenses in booking goods (or invoices or services) in and out, telephoning or corresponding about deficiencies and relationships between the staffs of the two companies are adversely affected.

Here again, confidence within the company as well as in its customers will be increased, if they can demonstrate that their processes conform to BS 5750 (ISO 9000).

In consequence, a commitment to Total Quality by the supplier offers him the opportunity not only to satisfy his customer but also to reduce his own costs, all or part of which he may wish to pass on to the buyer, to his own staff and/or increase his margins.

A further benefit to the supplier is the motivation of his own staff. As we have discussed in the chapter on Human Aspect (Chapter IX), achieving individual goals, satisfying customers and pride in one's own job and company are all factors which motivate people and a well motivated staff will be more able and willing to provide Total Quality to internal and external customers.

Most calculations of lack of quality only take into account the direct costs of materials and labour of producing the product; associated costs are often omitted and overheads are hardly ever included. The much less definable costs such as motivation of staff, image in the market and the impression created on the customer himself are even more difficult to gauge.

The potential of increasing business with the customer in question and with other potential clients must also be considered. An ever increasing number of buyers are shortlisting suppliers not only on the basis of price, product features and product quality but their decision is taken on the quality of the total offering of the supplier. Many manufacturers are buying as many components as they did in the past but they do so from fewer suppliers – suppliers have to qualify to be included on the list of potential suppliers. In some companies recognised total service standards (BS 5750 or ISO 9000) are required for a supplier to be included on a short-list; it would be difficult for a company who themselves conform to the tough standards required, to use suppliers who are not also conforming to these standards.

Benefits to the End User

The end user benefits by getting value for the money he spends on the product or service – customers are now much better informed of what is available on the market. They are hungry for high quality products and services and are willing to pay for them. They are not willing to put up with inefficient, uncaring and self-centred suppliers and they are increasingly able to choose suppliers who can deliver what they need.

The end user does not want to spend his time arguing with his supplier or the product's manufacturer about shortcomings of the product. Even if the supplier is bearing the cost of putting the fault right (e.g. under warranty), the customer loses time in negotiating with the supplier, often also losing the promised benefit of the product for a period of time.

What the customer really wants is to take a decision about what he wants to buy, and then have the product or service perform to the promised standards or better.

The result must therefore develop into a "Win-Win" situation.

The Need to Work for a Win-Win Situation

It is one thing to convince everyone along the way that Total Quality at all stages will be beneficial to the end-user, the manufacturer and to the sub-contractor. As in most agreements, the most long-term benefits will arise if all parties to the agreement gain from its implementation, i.e. that a "Win-Win" situation is reached.

It is quite another thing to put a programme like this into action. Too many businesses still regard the buying and selling process as an adversary situation with a winner and a loser. In more recent years many more long-term relationships between suppliers and buyers have developed. These new relationships have changed the methods by which suppliers and buyers develop projects. They communicate with each other at a much earlier stage to ensure that both parties are able to plan an efficient support for the end product. The project must be profitable to both parties, their developments must be in line with one another and they must be committed to each other. This means much greater disclosure of information to each other of sometimes quite sensitive data, including investment, product development etc.

But this happy end result is unlikely to happen by itself; both parties will have to do a great deal of work to change fixed attitudes and create a feeling of DISSATISFACTION with today's results. Whatever allows a company to be in a leadership position today will only be average in the near future. Every task can be done more effectively and everyone must be willing to accept that the excellent results of the present time can and must be improved upon.

The realisation of dependency on each other of supplier and buyer must lead to joint activities which will benefit both parties and, through them, the end user as well.

The drive must come from the top in both companies and the common purpose of both companies must be restated over and over again. The adversary buyer-supplier relationship mentioned earlier is so engrained that the new cooperative approach must be continually reinforced by creating joint working parties and common goals.

Management must move from fire-fighting to fire prevention - sufficient time must be found through this process for management of both companies to plan together for greater customer orientation throughout the chain of events.

This will require a continuous training and development process of management and staff at all levels. It will mean changing attitudes, acquiring additional skills and knowledge and learning to work together as a team. To optimise the end results will be the name of the game, not maximising individual departmental images.

All this will put a great deal of strain on the leadership qualities of management. It will have to change from the autocratic issuing of orders to a cooperative style of management to bring out the creative skills of all employees.

The important aspect is to set the ball rolling. Once the spirit of achieving customer satisfaction has been installed jointly by all people involved in the delivery process, it will gather speed with every success it attained on the way.

CHAPTER XIII

Marketing Total Quality to Customers

It may appear to be a superfluous activity to market Total Quality to customers – after all, they are the ones for whom the concept has initially been developed, so will they not realise immediately that we have gone out of our way to satisfy them by introducing Total Quality throughout our own and our suppliers' companies?

The quick answer to the above question is "No". Customers tend to be much quicker in observing deficiencies than they are in spotting improvements. In consequence, we have to market the improvements that we have introduced. As in all marketing and selling situations, it will not impress customers very much if we tell them that we have improved this or that widget in our product or bought this or that software program to facilitate our customer support activity. What will impress them is if we

Identify Customer Benefits

In other words, what the customer is interested in is "What does the change do for me?". If our projects have been developed with customers in mind and based on customer feedback or research and the Total Quality programme has taken all these aspects into account, it should not be too difficult to identify which of our activities will improve specific customer needs.

Keeping close to customers often makes it possible to identify customer needs which have not been explicitly stated and, at the same time, help the manufacturer. For instance, one of the manufacturers of bulk chemicals had the problem of his customers ordering large quantities at short notice to take advantage of quantity discounts. This placed a considerable strain on the scheduling of manufacture and a storage problem at the customer. By talking to the customers and changing the procedure, this manufacturer was able to negotiate yearly quantities with customers for regular delivery while at the same time allowing the customer some variation from the standard order. This overcame the manufacturer's scheduling problem, gave the customers the quantity discounts they needed, saved them storage space and simplified administration, as they only needed to notify the manufacturer if variation of order was required.

By knowing our customer requirements we can then explain to him how our internal improvements will benefit his own operation. At senior management level some of these benefits will only be known if we, the suppliers, will be able to demonstrate benefits to him. Senior management will be made aware by their own staff when a supplier delivers sub-standard products or services, makes errors in invoices or falls down on delivery promises. If everything works smoothly, the operating staff will know it but it is up to us to make it known to the decision maker that our products, services and support activities are all designed to satisfy his needs and that we have conformed to all standards.

Communicating Total Quality to Customers

One of the ways this is being done effectively by some companies is to arrange visits of management to each others' facilities. During these discussions it is possible to review past performance, the improvements that have taken place during the recent past and to examine how buyer and supplier can gain additional benefits by closer cooperation and, perhaps, even longer term commitments.

It is possible for the supplier to physically demonstrate to the buyer how the benefit he is getting has been achieved, e.g. by showing him the streamlined order handling, dispatching, and invoicing system that has been introduced and to show how support to this specific customer has improved over time by its use.

Another very effective way for the supplier to demonstrate the total quality of his offering is to provide customers with guarantees not only for the performance of the product but also for all support activities. In some industries penalty clauses for delays in delivery of products or services are widely utilised. It increases the confidence of the buyer in the reliability of his supplier, if this type of guarantee is offered without the customer demanding it.

Being able to demonstrate to customers that an independent organisation such as the British Standards Institute has examined its processes and is inspecting them at frequent intervals and certifying that the supplier is conforming to BS 5750 (ISO 9000) will also increase the customers' confidence.

The whole exercise of marketing Total Quality to customers is an image-building activity which should be made known to the market as a whole as well as to individual customers. In some instances, this public relations activity actually improves the supplier's performance by identifying remaining weaknesses in the system by improved customer feedback. An example of this was the commitment some two years ago by the car manufacturer Volkswagen (VW) to supply any spares for models after a certain date to anywhere in Germany within 24 hours. Naturally, VW only publicised this offer once they believed that they were achieving this target. In practice it was shown that they did fall down in some pockets of the country and the PR campaign ensured that VW was made aware very quickly by their customers of any instance when they fell down on their target.

Faint-hearted managers may find it an excessive risk to commit their company to publicly stated targets but if they genuinely believe that they can meet these goals, the public commitment will create the desired image in the market-place and motivate the company's own staff to strive to achieve these goals in every instance, i.e. to apply total quality in practice and show publicly the company's confidence in itself and its employees.

By announcing the company's commitment to tough quality goals in every field of its activities, the company is also setting an industry standard in the mind of customers which competitors will have to try and follow and our company may gain a marketing advantage by being the leader and, by striving for further improvements, stay ahead of the competition.

CHAPTER XIV

Total Quality – the Never Ending Task

Total Quality is unlike many other company programmes: most programmes have a beginning and an end – Total Quality is a company culture which does not have an end. A quality target sought for in the past is the standard of today and will be inadequate for tomorrow. Our support to internal and external customers can always be further improved and all of us should recognise that fact and be dissatisfied with what we are providing to our "customer" at present.

The Chairman of a major multi-national company who had driven Total Quality throughout his organisation had just explained to a group of financial analysts the initial investment that company had made in changing attitudes and activities and the considerably greater financial and operational benefits they had obtained from this approach. One of the analysts then asked whether the TQ programme was now completed. The Chairman replied: "Now that we have run this programme aggressively for five years I realise that we are beginning to scratch the surface of the issue".

This does not mean that individual projects within the Total Quality programme should not have specific targets for completion of work to an agreed goal. What it does mean is, that once this goal has been reached there are other peaks to be climbed.

The difficulty of management is to sustain the impetus of the drive for customer satisfaction through total quality over a long period of time. When a company is used as an example of excellence in all its activities, it is difficult to keep the creativity of the company's employees concentrated on further improving its quality and processes.

It is important that by the time a company has been recognised as one of the leaders in satisfying customer needs, the whole culture in the company has been directed towards a steady and continuous improvement of Total Quality. Each employee must feel free, able and motivated to innovate and contribute.

This feeling of freedom to innovate and contribute can only be achieved by management demonstrating its active and ongoing support for all employees willing to constructively criticise current products, processes and methods. Individual or group suggestions for improvements should be publicly recognised and a fair system of appraising proposals instituted. In addition to public recognition, many companies offer tangible rewards to the proposers but a study has shown that the number and quality of these suggestions is more dependent on the efficiency of the evaluation process than on the existence or value of the rewards.

Ability of employees to sustain the drive for Total Quality requires a good communication and feedback system throughout the company. It must give employees the opportunity to learn new skills and acquire additional knowledge to enhance their capabilities to contribute to the total process. Most employees are very willing to learn as long as the training process is not carried out in a threatening environment. The manpower development process must allow employees to grow to the limit of their abilities.

Motivation to innovate and contribute will be generated by an enthusiastic willingness to listen to employee suggestions, providing the necessary tools to carry out their studies and make the necessary tests and by communicating success stories throughout the company. It is management's responsibility to remove, or at least moderate, any obstacles in the way of releasing the intellect, experience and enthusiasm of their staff.

Management must realise that Total Quality is the task of everyone in the company, not only of creative or inventive members. It is a cooperative effort involving each function and the quality of the whole is only as strong as the weakest link in the chain of events. This should give everyone a vested interest not only to contribute to the limits of his ability himself, but to assist every colleague to do the same.

We should all remember that satisfying customers is not a spectator sport – every member of the company must feel it is his responsibility to contribute to "Customer Satisfaction through Total Quality".

A quote from Mr. Jack Welch, Chairman and Chief Executive of General Electric of the United States sums it up most effectively:

> "Customers will be judge, jury and executioner of any business that does not anticipate, satisfy and care about their needs".

Index

A *Career in* Professional Service Engineering

by John Wellemin

The service sectors of modern industrial countries have expanded at an unprecedented rate during the last decade. Careers in Service Engineering can be both lucrative and rewarding. This book is an invaluable aid to career choices and optimising success. The author, an experienced practitioner, looks in detail at the roles, background, career development, company training, and future of the Professional Service Engineer, showing in detail how to get started and succeed.

"This new book deserves to have a wide readership, particularly among school leavers and young adults who are seeking to know about opportunities of work and challenges offered in Service Engineering. The passages that set this role in the context of the company's overall operations and its profits is a refreshing change to the more narrow approach adopted by many authors of careers material. The chapter on career development could almost be made required reading for existing engineers and their managers."

Bryan Nicholson, Past-Chairman of the MSC. ISBN 0-86238-120-7

The Handbook of Professional Service Management

Caring for the Customer Before, During and After the Sale
by John Wellemin

This is an informative and readable book on the wide-ranging subject of Customer Service Management. It takes the reader from the purely technical after-sales support activity to the much broader role played by Service in running a business - in fact, a business within a business.

It covers all aspects of Service Management and its relationship to other functions, the customer and its own staff. It is arranged to be used as a reference book or for updating the reader's knowledge of the whole Service Management activity.

ISBN 0-86238-050-2

Quality - a challenge for everyone

by Kerstin Jonson

Everyone knows that quality is important. As consumers we demand it. For commercial enterprises it is a competitive tool. For both buyers and supplers quality needs to be achieved efficiently and at a reasonable cost.

Only comparatively recently has the quality objective begun to be seen as something to be pursued in all areas of a company's operation - not just in the area of manufacturing.

Every employee in every type of organisation has a role to play in the quality process and should be aware of what that role is and be committed to it.

This book covers from "what is quality?", and "why invest in quality" to "how to design a quality system" and "who is responsible?". It is aimed both at managers who care about the quality of the prduct, activity or service for which they are responsible, and their staff, whose understanding of and dedication to quality principles are vital to the ultimate success of the enterprise.

ISBN 0-86238-194-0

Quality control

a training package about quality for *all* employees

The aim of the course is to increase awareness of the overall importance of the concept of quality for the success of the company and consequently initiate processes of change in all employees with the aim of achieving the RIGHT quality for the products and services of the company. This is done by supplying knowledge of the activities that influence the product quality and increasing understanding of the fact that these activities are connected and can be controlled.

One of the most important features of this course is to improve cooperation between different departments. Tutors material consists of: instructions; five video cassettes; aworkbook; a textbook (see above). The course participants material is a workbook and textbook. **For further information contact Chartwell-Bratt Ltd, Old Orchard, Bickley Road, Bromley, Kent, BR1 2NE, Kent, Tel: 081-467 1956; Fax 081-467 1754**